D1713507

THE
MARTIN
LUTHER
TREASURY

edited by **ERWIN PAUL RUDOLPH**
Devotional writings from the man many call
"the greatest of the Reformers."

While this book is designed for the reader's
personal enjoyment and profit, it is also intended
for group study. A leader's guide is available
from your local bookstore or from the publisher
at $. 75.

VICTOR BOOKS

a division of SP Publications, Inc., Wheaton, Illinois
Offices also in Fullerton, California • Whitby, Ontario, Canada • London, England

Abridged from *Luther's Works*, Vol. 42, 43, and 51.
General Editor, Helmut T. Lehmann, Philadelphia:
Fortress Press, 1974. Reprinted by permission.

Recommended Dewey Decimal Classification: 242
Suggested subject headings: Reformation; Devotional Literature

Library of Congress Catalog Card Number: 79-64040
ISBN: 0-88207-518-7

VICTOR BOOKS
A division of SP Publications, Inc.
P.O. Box 1825 • Wheaton, Illinois 60187

Contents

Preface

These excerpts from Martin Luther's writings reveal the quality of intellect and conviction that led him to discountenance the practices of the established church and eventually to spur on the Reformation in Western Europe.

Luther was very much a man of his time. He was also very much a man of God. While he speaks from the context of his own culture, he emphasizes clearly the teaching of God's Word that he came to know so personally through arduous study. You will sense his devotional warmth in his writings.

Erwin P. Rudolph

Martin Luther, the Man
(1483-1546)

One day in July 1505, near the old city of Erfurt, Germany, a group of law students paused in front of an Augustinian monastery. One of their number, a lively, pleasant young man of 22, bade good-bye to his fellows and walked through the gate into the life of the cloister. Already a diligent student and conscientious follower of the church, Martin Luther felt the call of God to a holy and separated life. This was his way of renouncing the world and placing his life at the disposal of God. Beginning as a submissive servant of the Roman Catholic Church, this young man was to lead a powerful reformation of the church and revival of faith in evangelical Christianity.

Pre-Reformation Church

The state of the church in the years preceding the Reformation was deplorable. Since the time of Augustine there had been a continual contention for supremacy between the bishops of Constantinople and Rome. Till the ninth century, the Eastern or Greek Church was entirely separated from the West. Then in the eleventh century the pope of Rome established general authority, assuming a despotic power in both ecclesiastical and political areas.

The authority and infallibility of the pope became primary in Christian belief. Erroneous views prevailed about pilgrimages, purgatory, and celibacy. One of the most abused practices was that of indulgences. This belief held that all the good works of the saints that exceeded those necessary for their justification were deposited, together with the merits of Jesus Christ, in an inexhaustible treasury. St. Peter and his successors, the popes, were in charge of the keys and might open the treasury at will. Money was the usual inducement to open the storehouse to secure pardon for sins and release of a soul from purgatory.

Such indulgences began in the eleventh century when Urban II recompensed those who fought to rescue the Holy Land from the infidels. Gradually the awards were extended. The Roman Chancery published a book listing the precise sum to be charged for the pardon of each sin. Tetzel, a promoter of indulgences, went so far as to say as soon as the money "tinkled in the chest" the souls were released from the torments of purgatory.

In addition to these abuses, the Bible was not read by the laity nor well understood by many of the clergy. The lives of many parishioners were immoral. Some of the fictitious relics foisted upon the poeple were: a piece of earth from which the first man was made, a step of the ladder Jacob saw in a dream, a lamp of one of the foolish virgins, a piece of the sail used by St. Peter, and several instruments used in the crucifixion of Christ, including splinters from the cross.

Rome was the center of political intrigue, avarice, and homicide. Anything could be bought for a price, including the gifts of the Holy Spirit. The many errors and abuses brought into the church by the religious hierarchy pointed up the need for reformation of the pope and clergy. Accordingly, four general convocations or diets were held for that purpose: The first at Pisa, Italy (1409); the second at Constance, Switzerland (1414-18), where John Huss was burnt alive; the third at Sienna, Italy (1423); and the fourth at Basel, Switzerland (1431).

Some preparatory steps for a reformation had been taking place; many had already died for the faith. When Constantinople was taken by the Turks in 1453, many learned men were driven into Italy and Germany where they studied Hebrew, Greek, and Latin. And the invention of movable type in the mid-fifteenth century aided quietly the spread of reform literature—especially the Bible. The reformation task was not effectively performed, however, till Luther himself struck boldly and decisively against the prevailing oppression and abuses.

Luther

Martin Luther was born November 10, 1483, in Eisleben, Germany. His father, a miner, took care of the early education of his son, who was already showing signs of being a genius. At 18, he was sent to the University of Erfurt, ostensibly to study law, but his natural predilections were toward solitude and contemplation. Hence, he entered early the life of an Augustinian friar.

Knowledgeable in philosophy and theology, Luther applied himself to diligent study of the Bible. His assiduous study and learning brought him an invitation to teach in the University of Wittenberg, where he was later made a doctor and professor of divinity.

When his enemies questioned his authority to promote reformation, Luther pointed out that in taking his degree he had sworn not only to teach sound doctrine, but to defend its purity against heresy.

The Bible became for Luther the source of doctrine and the foundation of faith. With it he fearlessly defied his critics. He expounded many books, beginning with Paul's Epistle to the Romans, in which "the just shall live by faith" (1:17) impressed him deeply. He preached with unusual eloquence to listening multitudes. Commissioned in 1516 to visit the monasteries of the Augustinian orders, he recommended to the friars the reading of the Bible, with salutary results.

At this time Leo X, in an effort to increase the depleted revenues of the church, appointed Tetzel, a Dominican friar of dubious character, to sell indulgences in Saxony. When Luther opposed him, Tetzel preached publicly against Luther and all those who resisted the authority of the pope. On October 31, 1517, Luther published his Ninety-five Theses containing his beliefs about indulgences and challenged anyone to oppose them orally or in writing. These spread rapidly over Germany.

Leo summoned Luther to Rome but the latter declined, stating he preferred to be tried in Germany. The University and the Elector of Saxony interceded in his behalf for a trial in Augsburg on October 8, 1518. When asked to renounce his views concerning indulgences and faith as a prerequisite to receiving the sacrament, he replied he could not renounce opinions founded on reason and derived from Scripture. The court of Rome followed with a formal bull of excommunication June 15, 1520, in which he and his followers were condemned as heretics.

Although Luther did not design to overthrow the

whole church system, his discussions soon touched upon the idolatry of worshiping saints, vain trust in pilgrimages, and false views of purgatory. He was summoned again to appear at the Diet of Worms to account for his writings and opinions. His friends were apprehensive for his personal safety, but he replied, "Thither will I go and defend the truth in the name of the Lord." The unjust court consisted of the emperor, six electors, princes, dukes, bishops, ambassadors, and officers. Two questions were put to him: Would he acknowledge authorship of the writing ascribed to him? and Would he recant? Admitting he had written the works in question, he refused to retract his opinions stating, "Unless I am bound and forced in my mind by arguments which convey conviction to retract, it is not safe to do it. Here I am. I cannot! I dare not! I will not! So help me, God. Amen."

A few days later, an edict of the emperor instructed all princes not to defend or protect Luther or his opinions under penalty of high treason. Luther withdrew to Wartburg Castle, near Eisenach, where for nine months he published several treatises and translated the Bible into German. He married a nun from a noble family in 1526.

The name *Lutheran*, coined originally by an antagonist of Luther to refer to a dissenting sect, soon took on honorable connotations, although Luther was averse to using his name in the church in a divisive sense. The term *protestant* arose from the six evangelical princes and fourteen free and imperial states and cities who protested against the edict of Worms that no person be permitted to embrace the new "heresy" before the meeting of a general council.

A prominent friend of Luther, Melanchthon, drew up a confession of faith in the name of the protestants which was read at the Diet of Augsburg in 1530. Consisting of 28 articles, it was the first symbolical book of the Lutherans. A severe decree of the diet was issued against the protestants which encroached upon their ecclesiastical and civil liberties. After much confusion and numerous bloody battles, the protestant religion was established in Germany by the Treaty of Westphalia, 1648.

Luther died on February 18, 1546, at Eisleben, where he was born. He has been celebrated as the greatest Christian leader since the time of the Apostles. He carried on the great Reformation under heaven's protection against the most formidable powers on earth. He was determined to defend the cause of truth, liberty, and religious faith. He would not compromise with his enemies or resort to palliatives to cure evil; his aims were to strike at the root of prejudicial authority. Shortly before his death he was heard praying that the Lord would receive his soul and establish the kingdom of truth and peace after his death. The Lord honored his request, for his work flourished in the hands of those who followed in his train.

Teacher, Pastor, Counselor

Luther's career as a professor and reformer involved three areas of activity: as a teacher of theology, as a pastor and preacher, and as personal counselor.

Until he posted his Theses in 1517, Luther was a relatively obscure Augustinian monk, preacher, and professor at the University of Wittenberg. But by the end of 1521 he was the most controversial figure in Europe. During this time he wrote many devotional writings. These are free of polemic and draw heavily upon the Bible rather than the church fathers. Although restrained, they are intellectually and religiously advanced and provide an excellent illustration of literature that aims to lead the soul in its quest of godliness. These include *Meditations on Christ's Passion* (1519), *On Preferring to Die* (1519), *On the Worthy Reception of the Sacrament* (1521), and *Comfort When Facing Great Temptations* (1521). Those selected for inclusion here are *An Exposition of the Lord's Prayer* (1519) and *Fourteen Consolations* (1520).

Luther continued to write works of devotion to the year before his death. All of them evidence a deep pastoral concern. They are not polished literary masterpieces but were written in a "casual, epistolary style." Although the later works were usually written for a particular person, Luther was aware that they were for a wider audience. Always vigorous and direct, they summon to daily repentance and trust in God and defiance of Satan's cohorts, whether pope or Turk or prince. However, they are not bitter or vengeful and call for prayer for enemies and persecutors. Titles that illustrate the later devotional works are: *A Letter of Consolation to All Who Suffer Persecution* (1522), *That a Christian Should Bear His Cross with Patience* (1530), *Appeal for Prayer Against the Turks* (1541), *To the Saxon Princes* (1545).

Sermons

The Postils, published by Luther, constitute the only "sermons" which we have in his own hand. They are expositions and sermon helps on the Gospels and Epistles intended for preachers with inadequate theological training and for family reading.

From some outlines in his own hand we know how Luther prepared his sermons. There were key words and phrases which he jotted down as a guide, but when he preached he often departed from the outline or rearranged it in the pulpit, adding new ideas or leaving out sections. Hence, we have most of his sermons in the form of stenographic notes and versions worked up from such outlines. Yet many of the transcriptions are so complete that we have a reasonably accurate reconstruction of what was actually spoken.

Before 1521 Luther's sermons bore the influence of scholastic training and homiletics. Scholastic structure began with theme and a passage of Scripture. From this theme a proposition was developed and explained and supported by authorities. Emphasis was on logic and biblical authority, and the form was simple.

After 1521 Luther's preaching was expository rather than thematic or topical. It began with a text of considerable length and aimed to help the hearers to thoroughly understand it. The goal was always that God might speak to the hearer through the sermon. Sermons that follow a text, verse by verse, are called homilies. Luther did not bind himself to treat the text exhaustively. His sermons were often preached as running sermonic commentaries on the Bible. Some without texts dealt with the catechism, baptism, and the Lord's Supper.

These sermons still speak to readers today. One hears through them the voice of Christ. Compared with today's preachers, Luther may sound objective, but his concentration is on the Gospel and the vitality of the Christian life, not as a hermeneutical principle or homiletic method, but as an inner necessity. In one sermon he said, "When I preach a sermon, I take an antithesis." That is, he never proclaimed God's great affirmations without setting forth his reflections of man's presumption, work-righteousness, and mere reason. Luther's own personal struggle is felt in the sermons.

Worshipers the world over still sing with strong feeling the words of this man's Battle Hymn of the Reformation,

> A mighty fortress is our God,
> A bulwark never failing. . . .

Part I

An Exposition of the Lord's Prayer

When Christ's disciples asked Him to teach them how to pray, He replied, "In praying do not heap up empty phrases as the Gentiles do; they think they will be heard for their many words. Do not be like them, for your Father in heaven knows well what you need before you ask Him. Pray then like this, 'Our Father, who art in heaven, Hallowed be Thy name, etc.'" (Matt. 6:7-13)

From these words of Christ we learn about both the words and the manner in which to pray. Since our Lord is the Author of this prayer, it is without a doubt the most sublime, the loftiest, and the most excellent. Every absolution, all needs, all blessings, and all men's requirements for body and soul, for life here and beyond, are abundantly contained in it.

This prayer is divided into two parts. The first consists of a preface or introduction, the second of seven petitions.

The Introduction: Our Father Who Art in Heaven

Of all names, there is none that gains us more favor with God than *Father*. To speak the words *Lord* or

God or *Judge* would not be nearly as gracious and comforting to us. The name *Father* is part of our nature and is sweet by nature. With this name we likewise confess that we are the children of God, which again stirs His heart mightily, for there is no lovelier sound than that of a child speaking to his father.

The words "who art in heaven" are also helpful, for they point out our miserable and pitiful condition which moves us to pray and God to have compassion on us. It says, as it were, "O Father, You are in heaven, while I, Your poor child, am in misery on earth, far away from You, surrounded by many mortal dangers and spiritual perils."

This lofty word cannot possibly issue from human nature, but must be inspired in man's heart by the Spirit of Christ, for no man is so perfect as to be able to say truthfully that he has no father here on earth—that God is his only Father. Our nature is so base that it always covets something here on earth and will not content itself with God in heaven.

The term "Our Father" refers to a confidence that we can place solely in God.

All teachers of the Scriptures conclude that prayer is nothing else than the lifting up of heart or mind to God. But if the lifting up of the heart constitutes the essence of prayer, it follows that everything else which does not invite the lifting of the heart to God is not prayer.

Indeed, no one should depend on his heart and presume to pray unless he is well trained in warding off stray thoughts. Otherwise the devil will thoroughly trick him and soon smother the prayer in his heart. Therefore we should cling to the words and with their help soar upward, until our feathers grow and we can fly without the help of words.

The First Petition:
Hallowed Be Thy Name

No petition is greater to pray than, "Hallowed be Thy name." But note that God's name is holy in itself and is not hallowed by us, for it is God who hallows us and all things.

To see how God's name is hallowed in us, we first ask how it is profaned and dishonored in us. In the first place, we misuse God's name for the purpose of sinning and second, when we steal and rob Him of His name. A holy vessel in church may be desecrated similarly in a twofold manner—first, when it is not used in the service of God but for human purposes, and second, if it is robbed and stolen.

The name of God is first profaned in us when we employ it for sinful ends and the detriment of our soul. Instances of this are witchcraft, exorcism, lying, swearing, cursing, deceiving. In brief, we profane God's name when we do not live as His children.

What the Children of God are Like

We call a child devout who is born of upright parents, who obeys and is like them in every respect. Such a child rightfully possesses and inherits property and the full name of his parents. Thus we Christians, through our rebirth . . . become children of God. And if we pattern ourselves after our Father and all His ways, all His goods and names are likewise our inheritance forever. It follows that God's children should be gentle, merciful, chaste, just, truthful, guileless, friendly, peaceful, and kindly disposed toward all, even toward our enemies. But whoever is wrathful, quarrelsome, envious, rancorous, unkind, unmerciful, unchaste; he who curses, lies, swears, defrauds, and slanders—that person truly defiles, blasphemes, and profanes the divine name in which he was gathered into the congregation of God.

The meaning of the term "to hallow" or "make holy" is nothing else than withdrawing something from misuse and dedicating it to its proper use, just as a church is dedicated and appointed solely to the service of God.

The Self-righteous Ones

Here we refer to the arrogant ones who regard themselves as righteous and holy and do not feel that they are profaning the name of God. While they dub themselves righteous and truthful, they freely and fearlessly pilfer and purloin God's name. Their self-complacency, inward boasting, bragging, and self-praise are their greatest and most perilous handicap. They soon forget that everything they have is a gift from God. This is bound to lead to judging, condemning, slandering, backbiting, and despising of others. Thus they strut in their arrogancy, becoming hard-hearted and devoid of all fear of God. God alone has the right to pass judgment; as Christ says, "Judge not, that ye be not judged" (Matt. 7:1). Furthermore, God's name alone is holy. We are all sinners before God, without any distinction.

Today the world is full of these pernicious spirits who blaspheme God's name more shamefully with their respectable lives than all others do with their evil lives. Those who would be better than other people, like the hypocrite in the Gospel (Luke 18:11), I call arrogant saints and the devil's martyrs. Blind to their own evil, they do not understand that God granted them more grace than others so that they might serve others with this grace. When these people hear that

God alone is worthy of honor, they put on a nice act and deceive themselves still more by saying that in all they do they strive only for God's honor, so thoroughly depraved they are!

There are some who recognize and deplore that they do not fully hallow God's name, who earnestly pray that they may do so, and who take seriously their wretchedness. To them God grants what they ask. And because they judge and condemn themselves, He absolves them and remits their shortcomings. Those unthinking, frivolous spirits who make light of their failings, will in the end discover how great their sin was to which they closed their eyes. They will be damned for the very thing which they supposed would most surely save them, for Christ says to the hypocrites that they will receive the greater condemnation because of their long prayers (Matt. 23:14).

This is the sum and substance of this petition: Oh dear Father, may Your name be hallowed in us; that is, I confess and am sorry I have dishonored Your name so often and that in my ignorance I still defile Your name by honoring my own. Therefore, help me by Your grace so that I and my name become nothing, so that only You and Your name and honor may live in me.

The Second Petition:
Thy Kingdom Come

The second petition does two things: it humbles us and it raises us up. It humbles us because it compels us with our own lips to confess our great and pitiable misery. But it raises us up because it shows us how to conduct ourselves in such abasement. Every word of God terrifies and comforts us; it breaks down and builds up;

it plucks up and plants again; it humbles and exalts (Jer. 1:10).

Those who confess that they impede God's kingdom and pray sorrowfully that this kingdom might still come to them will, because of their penitence and prayer, be pardoned by God. But, together with the tyrants and destroyers of His kingdom, He will surely and severely judge those brazen spirits who are indifferent to the state of the kingdom and who do not earnestly pray for it.

The Two Kingdoms

There are two kingdoms. The first is a kingdom of the devil. The Lord calls the devil a prince or king of this world (John 16:11), that is, of a kingdom of sin and disobedience. To the godly, that kingdom is nothing but misery and a vast prison, as we find foreshown in the sojourn of the Children of Israel in Egypt. They were compelled to cultivate the land, to toil and suffer much woe; yet they gained nothing but the death that was planned for them (Ex. 1:10-16). Thus, he who submissively serves the devil must suffer much, especially in his conscience, and yet, in the end, he will thereby earn nothing but everlasting death.

All of us dwell in the devil's kingdom until the coming of the kingdom of God. However, there is a difference. To be sure, the godly are also in the devil's kingdom, but they daily and steadfastly contend against sins and resist the lusts of the flesh, the allurements of the world, the whisperings of the devil. In that way God's kingdom unceasingly engages in combat with the devil's kingdom. And the members of the former are preserved because they, within themselves, fight against the devil's kingdom in order to enlarge the kingdom of God. It is they who pray this petition with words, hearts, and pious deeds.

The others dwell in this kingdom, enjoy it, and freely do the bidding of the flesh, the world, and the devil. They yield to the devil; they impair, yes, devastate God's kingdom. To that end they amass goods, build magnificent houses, and covet all that the world can bestow, just as though they wanted to remain here forever.

The kingdom of God is a kingdom of truth and righteousness, of which Christ says, "Seek ye first the kingdom of God and His righteousness" (Matt. 6:33). What is this kingdom of righteousness? It is the state when we are free from sin, when all our members, talents, and powers are subject to God and are employed in His service, enabling us to say with Paul, "I live, but it is no longer I but Christ who lives in me" (Gal. 2:20).

Thus the petition "Thy kingdom come" briefly declares: "Our Father, do not let us sojourn very long here on earth, so that Your kingdom may be consummated in us and we may be delivered completely from the devil's kingdom. But if it please You to let us live longer in this misery, grant us Your grace that we may begin to build and constantly to increase Your kingdom in us, but reduce and destroy the devil's kingdom."

Two great errors are involved in this matter. The first is committed by those who run hither and yon for the purpose of becoming righteous, of entering God's kingdom. However, they refuse to face the true issue: they will not give their inmost self to God and thus become His kingdom. They perform many outward works which glitter very nicely, but inwardly they remain full of malice, anger, hatred, pride, impatience, and unchastity. It is against them that Christ spoke when He was asked when the kingdom was coming.

"The kingdom of God does not come with outward signs or appearances; for behold, the kingdom of God is within you" (Luke 17:20-21).

The other error made by many who pray this petition is to think of nothing but their own eternal bliss. Inspired by their carnal sense and by their dread of hell, these people are unaware that God's kingdom consists of nothing other than piety, decency, purity, gentleness, kindness, and of every other virtue and grace. They do not know that God must have His way in us—that He alone must be, dwell, and reign in us. We are saved only when God reigns in us and we are His kingdom.

The Third Petition: Thy Will be Done on Earth as It is in Heaven

This petition has the same twofold effect as the preceding one: it humbles and exalts.

In the first place, we judge and accuse ourselves with our own words, declaring that we are disobedient to God and do not do His will. For if we really did His will, this petition would not be necessary.

Since we find it necessary to pray this petition until our death, it follows that we are also found to be guilty of disobedience to God's will until our end. Who, in the face of our conviction by our own prayer, could be so arrogant as to deny that if God were to deal with us according to His justice, He should reasonably condemn us at any time for the disobedience which we have confessed with our own lips? This petition brings about genuine humility and a fear of God.

Again, having known and judged ourselves, we do not despair before God's judgment seat; rather we seek refuge in God's mercy. He who humbly confesses his disobedience and sin, and sincerely asks God for mercy, is righteous before God.

What a hard rebuff this petition is to our fleeting and wretched life, marking it as nothing but disobedience to the divine will. He who reflects deeply on this can truly have but little love for this life. He who does love such a life betrays that he does not in the least understand the Lord's prayer or the perils of his life.

What does it mean to say that God's will is done, or that it is not done? That God's will be done means nothing else than that His commandments are kept, for through these God has revealed His will to us. To understand God's commandments is to distinguish the old self, the old Adam in us, which leans toward wrath, hatred, unchastity, greed, vainglory, and the like. These evil impulses were born in us. From these stem all kinds of evil deeds such as murder, adultery, robbery, and similar transgressions against God's will.

The old Adam is mortified in two ways so that God's will may be done. First, he is mortified by us when we subdue and suppress our base impulses. There is nothing so dead to man and so hard to surrender as his own will. Many people perform fine works, but they completely follow their own inclinations. They are of the opinion that their will is good and true and that they do not in the least need this petition.

In the second place, this petition mortifies us through other people who antagonize us, assail us, disquiet us, and oppose our will in every way. They are the ones through whom God breaks our will so that His will may be done. That is why Christ says in Matthew 5:25, "Make friends quickly with your accuser." That is, we must surrender our will and accept our adversary's will as good, for in that way our will is broken. In the breaking of our will God's will is done.

Subjection of the Will

To understand this, we must note the ways in which our will is evil. In the first place, our will may be openly and undisguisedly evil and we must ask God's help in opposing it. Secondly, our will may be cloaked and disguised as something good. These are they who fly in the face of the supposed injustice or folly done them or others. Whatever they undertake must succeed. When thwarted they raise the hue and cry that their good will was frustrated. But if they would look at the matter in the light of day, they would discover that they were looking only to their own advantage and honor, their own will and opinion. A definite sign of an evil will is that it will not brook opposition.

In addition to these two evil wills there is a just and good will which also must not be done. David had such a will when he wanted to build a temple to God. Such was the will of Christ in the garden when He was reluctant to drink the cup; His will, though good, did not prevail. Likewise, if you willed to convert the whole world, raise the dead, lead yourself and all others to heaven, and to perform every miracle, you should still first consult God's will and subordinate your will wholly to His. God very often breaks this good will in His saints to prevent a false and evil "good" will from establishing itself through the semblance of good and to help us learn that no matter how good our will may be, it is immeasurably inferior to God's will.

This good will in us must also be hindered for its own improvement. God's purpose in thwarting our good will is to make it a better will. And this is done when it subordinates itself to the divine will.

That is what is meant by genuine obedience, a thing which, unfortunately, is unknown in our day.

You may say, "Did God not endow us with a free

will?" I reply: To be sure. But why do you want to make it your own will? Why not let it remain free? If you do with it whatever you will, it is not a free will, but your own will. God did not give you or anyone else a will of your own. Your own will comes from the devil and from Adam, who transformed the free will received from God into his own. A free will does not want its own way, but looks only to God's will for direction. By so doing it then also remains free, untrammeled and unshackled.

Hence, in this petition God bids us to pray against ourselves, for we are our greatest enemy. We see that our will is the most formidable element in us, and against it we must pray, "O Father, break my will and let my life be governed by Yours." Such a petition is painful to our human nature, for our own will is the most deep-rooted evil in us.

Therefore, we are asking for nothing else in this petition than the cross, adversity, and sufferings of every kind, as these serve the destruction of your own will.

The first three petitions are related to each other. The first asks that God's name be honored and that His glory and honor may dwell in us. But no one can attain to that unless he is righteous and lives in the kingdom of God. And no one is godly unless he is free of sin. Only he is free of sin whose own will is uprooted and replaced by God's will alone.

The Fourth Petition: Give Us This Day Our Daily Bread

Until now we used the little word *Thy.* But now we shall speak of *our, ours, us,* etc. We want to find the reason for this.

When God hears us in the first three petitions and hallows His name in us, He incorporates us into His kingdom and pours into us His grace. As soon as this grace starts to do God's will, it encounters a resisting Adam. Thus St. Paul laments in Romans 7:19 that he does not do what he wants very much to do. Then the grace in our hearts cries to God for help against this Adam and says, "Thy will be done," for man finds himself heavily burdened with his own self.

When God hears this cry, He resolves to come to the aid of His precious grace and to enlarge His newborn kingdom. He attacks the arch-knave, the old Adam, and blinds him and foils him on every side. This occurs when God visits all kinds of woe and grief upon us. Slanderous tongues and evil, unfaithful men are the means for this. And when such men are not adequate, the devils themselves have to serve this end. All this takes place so that our will may be throttled with all its evil inclinations and God's glory prevail.

When this happens, man finds himself beset by great fear and anxiety. He even imagines he has been abandoned and that there is no longer a God in heaven who cares to hear him. Then the real hunger and thirst of the soul make themselves known as the soul yearns for solace and help. This hunger is far more tormenting than physical hunger. Now the word *our* comes into its own; now we long to satisfy our need, and we say, "Give us this day our daily bread."

Strength in Tribulation

But how is that done? God has allotted us much tribulation in the world, and has offered us no other consolation than what Christ promised. "In the world you will have tribulation, but in Me you will have peace" (John 16:33). If you are willing to have God's kingdom come to you and have God's will be done, the more adversity you experience, the better is God's will done; this is especially true in the hour of death. It has been ordained—and no one can alter this—that in this world we find unrest, and in Christ we find peace.

In this tribulation the evil people are separated from the good. The evil people, who soon fall from grace and defect from the new kingdom of God, do not know the purpose of their tribulation or how to conduct themselves in it. The righteous are wise and well aware of the purpose of the divine will in spite of adversity. But this petition teaches where you may find solace and how you may find peace in such disquietude. You must say, "O Father, give us our daily bread." That is to say, "O Father, with Your divine Word comfort me, a poor and miserable wretch. I cannot bear Your hand, and yet I know that it works to my damnation if I do not bear it. Therefore, strengthen me, my Father, lest I despair."

It is only the Word of God or our daily bread that must strengthen us. That is what God says through Isaiah 50:4, "The Lord has given me a wise tongue so that I may know how to sustain them that are weary." And in Psalm 119:28 David says, "Strengthen me with Thy Word" and again in Psalm 130:5, "My soul has relied on His Word." With such teachings the Scriptures are full.

Christ the Bread

By whom does the Word come to us? It may come to us by a person—such as a pastor or someone else who lets us hear a comforting and strengthening word. Or it may come to us directly, as when God pours His Word into the heart of a suffering person, imparting strength to endure all.

The first word is *our*. Here we are not asking primarily for ordinary bread, which is also eaten by the heathen and given unbidden to all men. But it is *our* bread because we are children of the heavenly Father.

The second word is *daily*. It specifies a supernatural bread, since God's Word does not nourish man naturally in his mortal frame. It nourishes him as an immortal and supernatural being. Christ says, "He who eats this bread will live forever" (John 6:51, 58). Hence this petition means to say, "Father, give us the supernatural, immortal, eternal bread."

It is also called a select, tender, and dainty bread. In the Wisdom of Solomon 16:20 we read that this heavenly bread "is suited to every taste." Thus our heavenly bread is much nobler, finer, and more delicious and abounding more in all grace and virtue than natural bread.

In Hebrew this is also called "the bread for tomorrow." The Hebrew language uses the word *tomorrow* when we Germans use the word *daily*. In German the term *daily* refers to that which we have on hand ready for use, even though it is not used continuously. Thus the Hebrew meaning of the prayer is that God may give us the supernatural bread daily so that we have it on hand and are constantly supplied with it against the time of need and suffering, so that it might strengthen us, lest we despair for want of it.

The third word is *bread*, since it nourishes and strengthens the soul. The term is not to be understood in its narrow sense. Just as Scripture uses the physical bread to designate all sort of precious bodily food, so also the spiritual bread encompasses the innumerable kinds of food for the soul. There is a diversity of souls on earth and each has its own need. Yet the Word of God satisfies the needs of all.

The bread, the Word, and the food are none other than Jesus Christ our Lord Himself. Thus He declares in John 6:51, "I am the living bread which came down from heaven to give life to the world." So let no one be deceived by false appearances. Sermons and doctrines which do not show us Jesus Christ are not the daily bread and nourishment of our souls.

The fourth word is *give*. No one can obtain the bread, Jesus Christ, by himself, nor by studying, hearing, asking, searching. If we are truly to know Jesus Christ, then all books fall short, all teachers are too feeble, all reason is too limited. The Father Himself must reveal Him and present Him to us; as Christ states in John 6:44, "No one can come to Me unless the Father who sent Me draws him."

Now Christ our bread is given in a twofold manner. In the first place, outwardly, by persons, such as priests or teachers. This is done through words or through the Sacrament of the Altar. In the second place, Christ our bread is given us inwardly when taught by God Himself. You may ask, "What does it mean to know Christ?" You comprehend this fully when you realize that all your wisdom is damnable stupidity, your righteousness damnable unrighteousness, your purity damnable impurity, your redemption miserable damnation; and when you thus discover that before God and all creatures you are actually a fool.

The fifth word is *us*. Here every person is admonished to embrace all of Christendom in his heart and to pray for himself and for all man, especially for the members of the clergy whose duty is to administer the Word of God. If the priesthood and the Word of God are true to their purpose, then Christendom will prosper. A prayer spoken only in behalf of oneself is not a good prayer. Christ taught us to pray "our Father" and not "my Father," "give us this day our daily bread" and not "my daily bread." He wants to hear the throngs and not me or you alone, or a single isolated Pharisee.

The sixth word is *this day.* Since we live here amid perils and always in expectation of all kinds of suffering, such as the agony of death and the pain of hell, fear will prompt us to pray that God may not long delay His Word, but may be with us today, now. Therefore we do not say *tomorrow* as if today we were secure. It is also better to say *today* than *tomorrow* when God's will is about to be done and our own will dies in agony. At such a time the word *today* is almost inadequate, and we would wish that the bread be given us in this very hour and not merely today.

In summary, the petition means to say, "O heavenly Father, since no one likes Your will and since we are too weak to have our will and our old Adam mortified, we pray that You will feed us, strengthen and comfort us with Your holy Word, and grant us Your grace that the heavenly bread, Jesus Christ, may be preached and heard in all the world, that we may know it in our hearts, and so that all harmful, heretical, erroneous, and human doctrine may cease and only Your Word, which is truly our living bread, be distributed."

But do we not pray also for our physical bread? Yes, this too may well be included in this petition. However, this petition refers principally to Christ, the spiritual bread of the soul. This is why Christ teaches us not to worry about our body's food and raiment, but to take thought only for the needs of each day (Matt. 6:34).

It is indeed a good exercise in faith to ask God only for today's bread. This does not mean that we should not work for our daily needs or food but that we should not worry that we might starve unless we fear and fret. Our toil must be motivated more by our desire to serve

God through it, to avoid idleness, and to fulfill God's command to Adam, "In the sweat of your face you shall eat bread" (Gen. 3:19), rather than by our worrying over our nourishment.

The Fifth Petition: "And forgive us our trespasses, as we forgive those who trespass against us."

Take a look at the mightiest letter of indulgence that ever came to earth—one which cannot be bought with money but is free to everyone. Now you need not hasten to Rome or to Jerusalem or to St. James in quest of indulgence; now the poor can obtain this as well as the rich, the sick as well as the healthy, the layman as well as the priest, the servant as well as the master. This letter of indulgence reads, "If you forgive them their trespasses, your heavenly Father will also forgive you . . ." (Matt. 6:14-15).

There are two classes of people who cannot pray this petition and who cannot obtain this great indulgence. The first are blind to their own sin and so magnify that of their neighbor that they can declare impudently, "I will not and cannot forgive him." They have a beam . . . in their own eye, but they fail to see it. That is, they pay little heed to the sins they commit against God, but the sin of their neighbor weighs very heavy in their balances. For such people this petition becomes a sin, as we read in Psalm 109:7, "Let this prayer be counted as sin before God."

The others are more subtle. They are those who are offended spiritually by their neighbor. These sensitive and tender saints cannot stand sin and folly. These are the miserable saints who do not come to forgive or forget their neighbor's sin. It is in their nature never to be well-disposed in their heart toward any person. Thus they not only never become worthy of God's forgiveness, but God's displeasure with them will not even let them recognize their sin. Then they preen and say, "Indeed, I am not saying this to injure my neighbor, nor with any evil intent. I wish him everything good." O you hypocrite and charlatan! If you really were your neighbor's friend, you would keep silent and not spread his misfortune with such relish.

Humility Enjoined

Ponder whether you would like to have God deal with you as you deal with your neighbor. If you really want to do something about your neighbor's sin, then observe the precious golden rule of Christ when He says, "If your brother sins against you, go and tell him his fault, between you and him alone" (Matt. 18:15). Note that you are not to tell other people about it, but to keep it between him and you alone.

This widespread vice of backbiting and judging the sins of others is just about the most accursed sin on earth. And take note of this: the greater one's delight in sin, the greater the sin. Therefore, he who is fond of yelping and backbiting is no man's friend; in fact, he is a common enemy of mankind, just like the devil.

Thus we are admonished to learn not only that we are sinners against God, but that there are those who sin against us.

In the first place, we are gross sinners. Very few of us have not committed great and grave sins. Even if one has not, he still constantly falls short of satisfying God's commandments. He is unable to praise God sufficiently for his life, health, honor, possessions, friends, intellect, and innumerable other blessings from God. The fact that no one is so pious as not to have in himself some odor and leaven of the old Adam, is enough reason for God justly to reject man. Humility alone, therefore, will preserve even those who live in grace. Their sins will not be imputed to them if they denounce their sins, ask for mercy, and forgive their debtors.

The Sixth Petition: "And lead us not into temptation . . ."

If the word *temptation* were not in such general use, it might add to the clarity of this petition to say, "And lead us not into trials." This petition brings to our attention the miserable life that we lead here on earth. It is nothing more than one great trial. He who seeks peace and security here acts unwisely, for he will never find them. Though we all strive for them, it is still futile. This is and will ever remain a life of trials.

Therefore, we do not say, "Spare us the trial," but "Do not lead us into it." It is as if we were to say, "We are surrounded on all sides by trials and cannot avoid them; however, dear Father, help us so that we do not fall prey to them and yield to them, and thus be overcome and vanquished."

Thus, as Job asserts, this life is nothing but combat and struggle against sin. That dragon the devil assails us constantly, bent on swallowing us with his jaws, prompting St. Peter to say, "O dear brethren, be sober; be watchful. Your adversary the devil prowls around like a roaring lion, seeking someone to devour" (1 Peter 5:8). St. Peter here tells us that our enemy lies in wait for us, not only in one place, but everywhere. In other words, he says that all our members and senses hinder us, lure us on, and move us to unchastity, anger, pride, greed, and the like—inwardly by evil thoughts, outwardly with words and deeds. As soon as we notice this we must quickly lift our eyes to God and pray, "O my God and Father, defend and help me; do not let me succumb and be ensnared." O how blessed is he who properly repeats this petition!

Discipline of Trial

There are two kinds of trials. One comes on the left side. It is the trial that incites us to anger, hatred, embitterment, aversion, and impatience and includes sickness, poverty, dishonor, and all that distresses us especially when our will, plan, opinion, counsel, words, and deeds are rejected and ridiculed. These are common and daily occurrences in this life and are imposed by God through evil men or devils. When we experience these things we must act wisely, and not be surprised, for they are natural to this life. Then we must draw upon prayer . . . saying, "O Father, this is surely a trial ordained for me. Help me lest it entice and assail me."

In such a trial a man can play the fool in two different ways. In the first place, he plays the fool when he says, "Yes, I will indeed be pious and refrain from anger as long as I am left in peace." There are some who do not give our God and His saints any peace till He delivers them from the trial. God is then supposed to heal the leg of the one, make another rich, and help a third in his legal affairs. He is supposed to do what they want even if He has to extricate them from the trials at the expense of others.

Those who do not overcome this trial and also are not relieved of it go their way in anger, hatred, and impatience. The trial has defeated them, and now they yield to every base impulse. The devil has complete power over them, and they call upon neither God nor His saints.

The other trial is found on the right hand. It is the trial that lures us to unchastity, lust, pride, greed, and vainglory to all that appeals to our human nature. It is especially strong when people let us have our way, praise our words, our counsels, and our deeds. This is the most pernicious trial. It has gained the upper hand today, for the world strives only after wealth, honor, and pleasure. It is particularly the youth who no longer learn to contend against carnal lust and temptation. The whole world is filled with stories and songs about wenching and harlotry as though that were perfectly right. This all is a sign of the terrible wrath of God who permits the world to fall into temptation because no one implores Him for help.

But why does God let man be thus assailed by sin? So that man may learn to know himself and God. To know himself is to learn that all he is capable of is sinning; to know God is to learn that God's grace is stronger than all creatures. Thus, he learns to despise himself and to praise God's mercy. There have been people who tried to resist unchastity with their own strength, but they accomplished nothing, though they deceived their own bodies. Evil passions are extinguished only by the heavenly dew and rain of divine grace. Fasting, work, and vigils are necessary, but in themselves are not sufficient.

After God has forgiven us our trespasses, nothing is so important as being on guard against a relapse. We must sincerely and unceasingly say, "Father, lead me not into trials. I do not ask to be relieved of all trials, but I do entreat You not to let me fall and sin against my neighbor or against You." Thus St. James says, "My brethren, if many trials assail you, you must rejoice because of it" (James 1:12). Why? Because trials keep a man alert, perfect him in humility and patience, and make him acceptable to God as His dearest child. Blessed are they who take this to heart, for unfortunately, everyone today seeks tranquility, pleasure, and comfort in his life. Therefore, the rule of Antichrist is coming closer.

The Seventh and Last Petition: "But deliver us from evil."

Note that deliverance from evil is the very last thing that we do and ought to pray for. Under this heading we count strife, famine, war, pestilence, plagues, even hell . . . in short, everything that is painful to soul and body. Though we ask for releases from all this, it should be done in a proper manner and at the very last.

Why? There are some, perhaps many, who honor and implore God and His saints solely for the sake of deliverance from evil. They have no other interest and do not think of the first petitions which stress God's honor, His name, and His will. Instead, they seek their own will and completely reverse the order of this prayer. They are set on being rid of their evil, whether this redounds to God's honor or not.

An upright man, however, says, "Dear Father, evil and pain oppress me. I suffer much distress and discomfort. I am afraid of hell. Deliver me from these, but only if this is to Your honor and glory and if it agrees with Your divine will. If not, then Your will, and not mine be done" (Luke 22:42). That is a pleasing and good prayer and is certain to be heard in heaven.

Since, then, this life is nothing but one accursed evil in which trials are sure to emerge, we should pray for deliverance from evil so that trials and sin may cease and that God's will may be done and His kingdom come, all to the glory and honor of His holy name.

Amen!

The little word *Amen* is of Hebrew origin. In German it means that something is most certainly true. It is good to remember that this word expresses the faith that we should have in praying every petition. If we conclude our prayer with the word *Amen*, spoken with confidence, it is surely sealed and heard.

Before a person begins to pray he should examine himself to ascertain whether he believes or doubts that his prayer will be fulfilled. If he finds that he doubts or that he prays at random, the prayer is nothing. His heart is not constant. It is impossible for God to put anything into such a heart, even as you cannot drop anything into a person's hand if he does not hold it still.

Imagine how you would like it if a person were to entreat you earnestly and then conclude by saying, "But I do not believe that you will give it to me," although you would surely have given it to him! You would regard his petition as mocking. How, then, can we expect it to please God, who promises to grant our petition, when our doubt gives Him the lie, when in our prayer we act contrary to the prayer, when we insult His truthfulness which we invoke in our prayer?

Therefore, the little word *Amen* means the same as truly, verily, certainly. It is a word uttered by the firm faith of the heart. It is as though you were to say, "O God and Father, I am convinced that You are truthful, that You cannot lie. It is not the worthiness of my prayer, but the certainty of Your truthfulness that leads me to believe this firmly. I have no doubt that my petition will become and be an Amen."

In this respect some fail disastrously in prayer. They nullify it, for they utter it merely with their lips and not with their hearts because they will not believe that they are heard until they imagine that they have prayed well and worthily. Thus they build on themselves. Therefore, take note that a prayer is not good because of its length, devoutness, sweetness, or its plea for temporal or eternal goods. Not your zeal, but God's Word renders your prayer good. And only that prayer is acceptable which breathes a firm confidence and trust that it will be heard because of the reliable pledge and promise of God.

Part II

Consolations:
Seven Evils Considered

(Written and dedicated to Prince Frederick, Duke of Saxony, when he was stricken with a grave illness.) From the letter of dedication, "I realize that as one of your Lordship's subjects, I should share in your Lordship's illness together with the rest of your subjects, and suffer with you as a member with its head (Rom. 12:5) on whom all our fortunes, all our safety and happiness depend. . . . The book is not meant to adorn the walls of churches, but to uplift and strengthen the pious heart of your Lordship."

Your subject,
Martin Luther, Doctor

In speaking of the consolation which Christians have, the Apostle Paul in Romans 15:4 writes, "Brethren, whatever was written, was written for our instruction, so that through the patience and comfort of the Scriptures we might have hope." In this passage he plainly teaches us that our consolations are to be drawn from the Holy Scriptures.

The first part will deal with the evils. First, we shall consider the evil within us; second, the evil before us; third, the evil behind us; fourth, the evil on our left

hand; fifth, the evil on our right hand; sixth, the evil beneath us; and seventh, the evil above us.

The First Image: The Evil Within Us

Whether man believes it or not, it is certainly true that no torture can compare with the worst of all evils—the evil within man himself. The evils within him are more numerous and far greater than any which he feels. If a man were to feel his evil, he would feel hell, for he has hell within himself. You ask, "How can that be?" The prophet says, "All men are liars" (Ps. 116:11), and again "Every man living is nothing but vanity" (Ps. 39:6). To be a liar and vanity is to be without truth and reality. And to be without truth and reality is to be without God and to be nothing. This condition in turn is to be in hell and to be damned.

Therefore, when God in His mercy chastens us, He shows us and lays upon us only the lighter evils, for God knows that if He were to lead a man to a full knowledge of his own evils, that man would die at once. He did, however, give a taste of this to some, of whom it is said, "He brings down to hell and brings back again" (1 Sam. 2:6).

What is it, then, that prevents us from feeling this true evil? God has so ordered things that man might not perish by seeing his innermost evils. God hides them and wants us to see them only by faith. Therefore, in the day of evils, remember the day of blessings. See what a great good it is not to know the whole of our evil. Be mindful of this good, and the evil that you feel will torment you less. On the other hand, in the day of good, be mindful of evil. The evil that you feel will then be less of a burden. In this life a man's freedom from pain is always greater than his pain. This is not because his whole evil is not present, but because the goodness of God keeps it hidden so that he neither thinks of it nor feels it.

Therefore, the first image becomes a consolation when a man says to himself, "Not yet, O man, do you feel your evil. Be glad that you do not have to feel it." When compared with the greatest evil, the small evil thus becomes light. It is this that others mean when they say, "I have deserved something far worse, even hell itself"—a thing so easy to say, but horrible to endure.

Although this evil is hidden deeply, it bears fruits which are clearly seen. These are the dread and uncertainty of a trembling conscience, when faith is assailed and a man is not sure whether he has a gracious God. The weaker a man's faith, the more bitter will be the fruit.

Beyond this, but part of the evils within us, are all those tragic experiences described by the Preacher when he refers again and again to "vanity and vexation of the spirit" (Ecc. 1:2, 14). How many of our plans end in frustration! How many of our hopes are dashed! Nothing is complete and perfect. This is why Job (7:1) calls the life of man "a trial."

Yet these do not cease being evils just because they are less sharply felt by us. But because they are always with us and always active they have lost something of their meaning; and because of the goodness of God, our thoughts and feelings about them are blunted.

The Second Image: The Future Evil or the Evil Before Us

It will lighten your present evil in no small degree if you will turn your mind to the future evils. These are so numerous, so varied, and so great that they have given rise to one of the principal emotions, fear.

No man is safe from the evils that befall any other, for what one has suffered another may also suffer. This applies to all the historic events and tragedies of all ages and to all the lamentations of the world. How great do you think will be the number of misfortunes that assail our possessions, our friends, and even our very mind, which, after all, is the main target of all evils?

These evils increase in power and intensity as a man rises to higher dignity and rank. Since misery, shame, and indignity can suddenly overtake a man of such an exalted estate, he must at all times be in dread of these evils. If none of these evils befalls us, we should consider this a gain and no small comfort in the evil that does in fact become our lot, and exclaim with Jeremiah, "It is of the Lord's mercies that we are not consumed" (Lam. 3:22). When none of these things happen to us, it is because the preventing right hand of the Most High surrounds us on all sides with great might and like a well. . . .

Were it to be that possibly none of these evils should come, nevertheless death, known as the greatest of all terrors, is certain to come. . . . There is no one who would not choose to submit to all other evils if thereby he could avoid the evil of death. Even the saints dreaded it, and Christ submitted to it with trembling fear and bloody sweat (Luke 22:42-44).

Christians have another reason for dreading the evils to come. It is that which the Apostle depicts in 1 Corinthians 10:12: "Let him who stands take heed that he does not fall." The faith is so very slippery and the foe so very powerful, aided as he is by all our evil desires and the pleasures and lusts of the world.

Besides this, the foe himself is a master in the art of doing us harm, of reducing and destroying us in a thousand different ways.

Such is our life that not for a moment are we safe in our good intentions. It is true that wherever there have been highminded men who gave deep thought to these infinite perils of hell, we see that in contemplation of life and death (that is, of all the evils mentioned before), they desired to die and be delivered both from the present evils and from the sins into which they might fall.

The man who does not prefer the evil of death to the evil of sin loves God his Father but little. God has ordained that this evil be brought to an end by death, and that death be the minister of life and righteousness.

The Third Image: The Past Evil, or The Evil Behind Us

The sweet mercy of God shines forth more brightly in this image than in the others and is able to comfort us in every distress. Never does a man feel the hand of God more closely upon him than when he remembers the years of his past life.

Here a man may see how often he has done and suffered many things. He gave little thought to them before they occurred or while they were happening, and only after all was over did he find himself compelled to exclaim, "How did these things happen to me when I gave no thought to them, or thought something very different?" This bears out the proverb, "Man proposes, but God disposes" (Prov. 16:9). That is, God turns things around and brings to pass something different from that which man planned. In this one respect alone it is not possible for us to deny that our lives and actions are under the guidance of the wonderful power, wisdom, and goodness of God.

Therefore, even if there were no books or sermons, our very lives, led through so many evils and dangers, would abundantly commend to us the tender goodness of God. Thus Moses says in Deuteronomy 32:10, "The Lord kept him as the apple of His eye, and led him about, and carried him on His shoulders."

Out of this conviction the exhortations in the Psalter were born: "I remember the days of old; I meditate on all Your works; I ponder the work of Your hands" (Ps. 143:5); "Surely I shall remember Your wonders of old" (Ps. 77:11); and, "I have remembered Your judgments, and I am comforted" (Ps. 119:52). These and other exhortations are all intended to teach us that since God was with us when we did not think so . . . we should not doubt that He is always with us, even when it seems that He is absent from us. He who upheld us in many times of need, even without our request, will not forsake us in a smaller affliction, even though He seems to do so. Thus He says in Isaiah 54:7, "For a brief moment I forsook you, but I will gather you with great mercies."

Who cared for us during the many nights that we slept? Who cared for us while we worked, played, or were busy with those many activities in which we gave little thought to ourselves? Our entire care is completely in God's hand alone, and only rarely are we left to our own care. Now and then God permits the latter to make us aware of His goodness that we might see the difference between His care and ours.

Why, then, are we anxious about a single peril or evil when our whole life witnesses that He has reserved us from so many evils without any effort on our part? To know this is to know the works of God, to meditate on

His works, and in our adversities to comfort ourselves by the remembrance of them (Ps. 143:5; 119:52).

The Fourth Image: The Infernal Evil, or the Evil Beneath Us

Until now we have seen in all the evils which surround us, only a few are permitted to assail us. Is it not a miracle to be struck only now and then by one of the countless blows aimed at us?

Of the evils beneath us, the first is death and the other is hell.

When we consider the varied and terrible deaths by which other sinners are punished, we shall easily see how great our gain is in that we suffer less than we have deserved. How many men are hanged, strangled, drowned, or beheaded, who perhaps committed sins much smaller than ours! Their deaths and misery are held up to us by Christ as an image by which we can see what we have deserved. In Luke 13:1-5 it is said when they told Him of the Galileans whose blood Pilate had mingled with their sacrifices, Christ answered, "Do you think that just because they suffered these things these Galileans were greater sinners than all the other Galileans? I say to you, no; but unless you repent, you shall all perish in like manner. . . ."

Furthermore, we must note here the many infidels, heathen, Jews, and children, who, if they had been favored with the advantages given to us, would not now be in hell, but in heaven, and would have sinned far less than we. . . . We see, therefore, how much praise and love we owe our gracious God in every evil of this life, for each is scarcely a drop of the evils which we have deserved and which Job compares to the sea and to the sand on the shore (Job 6:3).

The Fifth Image: The Evil on Our Left Hand

Here we must hold before our eyes the vast multitude of adversaries and wicked men. We must consider, first, how many evils they would have inflicted on our bodies, property, good name, and soul, but were unable to because of the province of God. The higher a man's position in life and the broader his rule, the more he is exposed to such persecution, intrigues, slander, and plots of his enemies. In all this we may again mark and feel the nearness of God's hand. Should we be surprised if now and then we are touched by one of these evils?

We should take note of the evils which these men themselves endured—not to exult over them, but that we may feel pity for them. Their plight is worse than ours, because in both in a bodily and spiritual sense they are outside of our fellowship.*

If we consider this rightly, we shall see how greatly we are favored by God in that we bear some slight bodily ill while in the kingdom of Christ and in the service of God. We ought not even to feel it, since we are in the midst of such rich blessings.

Inspired by the love and example of Christ, the saints are wont to pray for wicked men, even for their enemies.

You see how deep is the abyss of evils that is here opened up and how it is an opportunity for pity and compassion and for overlooking our paltry ills. What God permits us to suffer is nothing compared to what they suffer. The reason these things affect us so little is that our hearts are not able to see how great is the shame and misery of a man lying in sin—that is,

---

*i.e., the fellowship or communion of the church

separated from God and possessed of the devil.

Who is so hard of heart as not to sicken at the wretched sight of those lying at the doors of the churches and in the streets, with disfigured faces, their noses, eyes, and other members so hideously consumed with festering sores that the mind is terrified and the senses recoil from the sight?* Yet how many sinners there are in the world to each one of those wretched creatures! When we disregard those evils of our neighbors, it follows that our own evil, though it be trivial, will appear to us to be the only one and the greatest of all.

But even in regard to bodily ills, these people are worse off than we are. How can they find sweet and pure joys, even if they have obtained everything their heart desires, as long as their conscience can find no peace? Can there be an evil more dreadful than the unrest of a gnawing conscience?

In brief, when all the evils of the wicked are viewed in the right spirit, whether they belong to enemies or friends, a man will then not only forget his own evil, but it will seem to him as if he were not suffering at all. With Moses (Ex. 32:32) and the Apostle Paul, he would desire to die for them, to be separated from Christ and expunged from the Book of Life just so they might be set free.

The Sixth Image: The Evil on Our Right Hand

On the right hand are our friends whose evil makes our own lighter, as St. Peter teaches (1 Peter 5:9), saying, "Resist the devil in firm faith, knowing that the same

---

*Luther alludes to beggars and other unfortunates who beg alms in front of the churches.

sufferings are inflicted on your brethren in the world." The church in its prayers also petitions that, urged on by the examples of the saints, we might initiate the virtue of their sufferings. The church sings:

What torments all the saints endured

That they might win the martyr's psalm.

From such words and hymns of the church we learn that the feasts of the saints, their memorials, churches, altars, names, and pictures are observed and multiplied to inspire others by their example to bear the same evils which they also bore. Unless they are observed in this light, the cult of the saints cannot be free of superstition.

The finest treatment of this section of our *Consolations* is given by the Apostle in Hebrews 12:4-11: "Until now you have not resisted to the point of bleeding in your struggle against sin . . . my son, do not take lightly the chastening of the Lord, nor become weary when you are rebuked by Him . . . Endure your chastening, for in it God is treating you as sons . . . All chastisement seems at the moment to be not for our pleasure but to our sorrow, but hereafter it offers the peaceful fruit of righteousness to those who have been exercised by it."

There is no room here for the excuse that some have lighter and others heavier burdens to bear. To everyone is given temptation according to a measure and never beyond his strength. Paul says, "God is faithful, and He will not let you be tempted beyond your strength, but with the temptation will also make a way of escape so that you may be able to bear it" (1 Cor. 10:13). Therefore, where there is greater evil, there is also more divine help and a way of escape, so that the inequality of suffering appears to be greater than it really is.

Does not St. John the Baptist, whose beheading by

Herod we commemorate today,* shame and amaze us all? We must be amazed that so great a man, the forerunner of Christ, should have been put to death, not after a public trial, not on a false charge, nor for the sake of the people, but for the sake of a dancing girl, the daughter of an adulteress! The ignominious death of this one saint should make every one of our evils light. This man died as if unknown to God, man, and all creatures. Compared with such a death, what sufferings have we to boast of?

We thus see that all our suffering is nothing when we consider the nails, dungeons, irons, faggots, wild beasts, and countless tortures of the saints, and also when we ponder the afflictions of men now living, who in our lifetime endure the most grievous persecutions of the devil. There is no lack of men who suffer more intensely both in body and soul than we do.

But some may say, "My sufferings cannot be compared with the sufferings of the saints. I am a sinner and do not deserve to be compared with them. They suffered for their innocence, but I suffer for my sins. Little wonder that they bore everything so blithely." That is a very stupid statement. If you suffer because of your sins, then you ought to rejoice that you are being purged of your sins. Then, too, were not the saints also sinners? Whenever you suffer, it is either because of your sins or your righteousness. Both kinds of suffering sanctify and save if you will but love them. Thus there is no excuse that remains.

The Seventh Image: The Supernal Evil, or the Evil Above Us

Finally, let us lift up our hearts and ascend with the bride into the mountains of myrrh (Song 4:6). Here is

Jesus Christ, the Crucified, Head of all the saints, the Prince of all sufferers.

There is nothing, not even death, that His passion cannot sweeten. Thus the bride says, "His lips are lilies, letting sweet-smelling myrrh fall in drops" (Song 5:13). What resemblance is there between lilies and lips, since lips are red and lilies are white? It is said in a mystical sense, as if to say that Christ's words are clear and pure, without even a vestige of bloodred bitterness or malice, but only sweetness and mildness. Yet into them He drops precious and chosen myrrh (bitter death). These purest and sweetest lips have the power to make the bitterest death sweet and fair and bright and dear, for death (like precious myrrh) removes all of sin's corruptions at once.

How does this come to pass? It is when Jesus Christ, God's Son, has by His most holy touch consecrated and hallowed all sufferings, even death itself, has blessed the curses, and has glorified shame and enriched poverty so that death is now a door to life, the curse a fount of blessing, and shame the mother of glory.

If you caress and embrace as sweetest relics the robe of Christ, the vessels, the water jugs, and anything Christ touched or used or hallowed by His touch, why will you not much more rather love, embrace, and kiss the pain and evils of this world, the disgrace and shame which He not only hallowed by His touch but sprinkled and blessed with His most holy blood? The more so, since for you there are far greater merits and blessings in these sufferings than in those relics. In them victory over death, hell, and all sins is offered to you, but in those relics nothing at all.

Oh, if we could only see the heart of Christ as He was

---

*Beheading of John the Baptist was observed on August 29.

suspended from the cross, anguishing to make death contemptible and dead for us. How fervently and cheerfully He embraced death and pain for us timid souls who are horrified by death and pain. St. Paul says, "Consider Him who endured such hostility from sinners against Himself, so that you may not be weary or fainthearted" (Heb. 12:3).

If we have learned from the preceding images, those beneath and near us, to bear our evils with patience, then surely this last image, in which we are lifted above and outside ourselves into Christ and placed beyond all evils, should teach us that we ought not only to tolerate those evils, but love them, desire them, and seek them out. If such thinking is foreign to a person, it means that the passion of Christ still has little meaning for him.

In keeping with this image we must, therefore, absorb and consume whatever evils we may have to bear, so that they will not only grieve us, but will delight us. This will come true if this image finds its way into our heart and abides in the innermost affections of our mind.

Part III

Consolations:
Seven Blessings
Considered

The second part also consists of seven images, the opposite of the seven in the first part. Of these, the first represents the internal blessing; the second, the future blessing; the third, the past blessing; the fourth, the infernal blessing; the fifth, the blessing on the left hand; the sixth, the blessing on the right hand; and the seventh, the supernal blessing.

The First Image: The Blessing Within Us

What person is there who can count up only those blessings he has within himself? How great, first of all, are the gifts of the body! Beauty, strength, health, and the alertness of the senses!

More excellent than all of these are the blessings of the mind, such as reason, judgment, knowledge, eloquence, and prudence. In all these we should gratefully acknowledge the bountiful hand of God and should take comfort in our infirmity. We should not be surprised if among so many and great blessings there is some intermingling of bitterness. So intolerable is constant and unvarying sweetness that it has truly been said, "Every pleasure too long continued turns into loathing," and also, "Even pleasure itself turns into suffering." Because of the excessive abundance of good things, we are unable to enjoy only good things in this life without a tempering of evil.

What, then, is it that God would have us lay to heart, except that the cross is held in honor even among the enemies of the cross?

Daily in the mass we sing, "Heaven and earth are full of your glory"* (Isa. 6:3). Why do we sing this? Because of the many blessings for which God must be praised, although this is done only by those who see the fulness of them. As we said concerning the evils of the first image, a man's evils are only as great as his knowledge of them, so it is with his blessings. Though they rush in and crowd upon us from every side, they are only as great as we acknowledge them to be.

The most beautiful and instructive example of this image is furnished by Job, who after the loss of his possessions said, "If we receive good from the hand of God, why should we not also bear evil?" (Job 2:10) Truly this is a golden saying and a great comfort in the day of trial.

However, these bodily blessings are common to all. But a Christian has other and far better blessings within, namely, faith in Christ, of which it is said in Psalm 45:13, "The king's daughter is all glorious within; her clothing is of wrought gold." Just as we asserted of the evil in the first image that no matter how great the evil in man, it is not the worst possible for him, so we say now that the Christian is unable to see the greatest blessings within himself. To have faith is to have the Word and truth of God, and to have the Word of God is to have God Himself, the Maker of all. If all

---

* This is sung in the Sanctus of the mass

these blessings in their fulness were revealed to the soul, it would in a moment break free from the body because of its exceeding abundance of sweet pleasure. Since this life of ours cannot bear to have them revealed, God mercifully keeps them hidden until they have reached their full measure. It is like loving parents who at times give their children foolish little toys with which they lead their hearts to hope for better faith.

At times, nevertheless, these inner blessings break out, as when a person with a happy conscience rejoices in his trust in God, speaks openly about Him, hears His word with eagerness, and is ready and quick to serve Him, to suffer evil, and the like. These are all signs of the infinite and incomparable blessings hidden within, which, like a small spring, send forth tiny rills.

The Second Image: The Future Blessing, or the Blessing Before Us

Those who are not Christians find but little comfort in contemplating future blessings, since for them all things are uncertain. Although we make much ado about that famous emotion called hope, we are still always deceived. Christ shows us this in Luke 12:6-21: The man said to his soul, "I will pull down my barns and build greater, and I will say to my soul . . . take your ease, eat, drink, and be merry. . . ." The comment follows, "So is he who lays up treasures and is not rich toward God."

Yet God has not forsaken the sons of men, but comforts them with the hope that evils will pass and that good things shall come. Though they must remain uncertain about the future, they yet hope with a sure hope which sustains them in the meantime, lest falling into despair they are unable to bear up under the present evil. Hence, even this kind of hope is the gift of God. He does not want man to lean upon it, but rather to see it as a reminder of the firm hope which is in God alone.

Christians certainly have the greatest blessings of all awaiting them in the future. However, these are attained only through sufferings and death. They surely also rejoice in that common hope that the evil of the present will come to an end and that blessing will increase. But their chief concern is that their own particular blessing might increase, namely, the truth that is in Christ in which they advance day by day and for which they live and hope.

But besides this blessing they have, as I have said, the two greatest blessings in their death.

The first is that through death the whole tragedy of this world's ills is ended. Whether he lives or dies, the Christian is always in a better state. That is why Paul says, "For me to live is Christ, and to die is gain" (Phil. 1:21). Again he says, "If a man lives, he lives unto the Lord; if he dies, he dies unto the Lord. Whether we live, therefore, or die, we are the Lord's" (Rom. 14:8). This security Christ has won for us by His death and resurrection. It is a great thing that death, which to others is the greatest of evils, is made the greatest gain for us. Like a slain serpent, death still has its former terrifying appearance, but now this is only a mask, for it is now a dead and harmless evil.

The other blessing of death is that death not only puts an end to the evils of this life's punishments, but that death also—which is even more excellent—puts an end to all sins and vices. As we have said already, this renders death far more desirable for believing souls than the former blessing, since the evils of the soul, namely, its sins, are incomparably worse than the evils of the body. This alone should make death desirable. If it does not, it is a sign that we neither feel nor hate the sins of our soul as we should. With slippery sins besetting us on all sides, our life is so full of perils that we are unable to live without sinning. Thus death is indeed the greatest blessing as it delivers us from these perils and cuts sin fully away from us.

Thus death, which for man was the punishment for his sin, has for the Christian been made the end of sin and the beginning of life and righteousness. Therefore, he who loves life and righteousness must not hate, but rather love death, if he desires to attain to either life or righteousness. Let him who is not able to do this pray God to enable him to do it. To this end we are taught to pray, "Thy will be done," because we cannot do this ourselves, since in our fear of death we love death and sin rather than life and righteousness.

It is true that through the envy of the devil death entered into the world, but it is evidence of God's surpassing goodness that after death entered, it is not permitted to harm us, but is taken captive from the very beginning and appointed to be the punishment and death of sin.

The Third Image: The Past Blessings, or the Blessings Behind Us

The consideration of this image is easy since it is made in contrast to the evils of the past. The Psalmist said, "Lord, You have searched me; You have understood my thoughts from afar, You have known my path and my lying down" (Ps. 139:1-3). It is as though he said, "I see now that whatever I have ever thought or done, whatever I shall attain or possess will not be the result of my labors but because long ago it was ordered by

Your solicitude for me, since You have foreknown all my ways."

We learn this from our own experience. When we reflect on our past life, is it not amazing that we thought, desired, did, and said many things that we were not able to foresee? How very different our course would have been if we had been left to our own free will. Only now do we understand God's ever-present care and providence over us, so that we were able neither to think nor speak anything except as He gave us leave. Thus it is written in the Wisdom of Solomon 7:16, "In His hands are both we and our words," and by Paul, "who works all things in me" (1 Cor. 12:6).

Thus we see how divine compassion and comfort sustain us. Still we doubt, even despair, that He cares for us today. So many examples offered to our foolishness and hardness of heart ought well to fill us with deep shame, if we ever doubt that the slightest blessing or evil can come to us without the particular providence of God. Thus St. Peter says (1 Peter 5:7), "Cast all your cares upon Him because He cares for you." Psalm 55:22 says, "Cast your burden on the Lord and He will sustain you; He will never suffer the righteous to be moved."

If only a man could see his God in such a light! How happy, how calm, how safe he would be!

However, if we fail to do this and then presume to care for ourselves, what else are we then doing but seeking to obstruct God's care for us, and at the same time creating for ourselves a life of sorrow and labor. And it is so futile! We accomplish nothing good thereby, as the Preacher says, "It is vanity of vanities, and vexation of the spirit" (Ecc. 1:2, 14). He finally came to the conclusion that it is a gift of God when a man may eat and drink and live joyfully with his wife—

when he passes his days without anxiety and commits his care to God.

Therefore, we ought to have no other care for ourselves except that we do not care for ourselves or rob God of His care for us.

The Fourth Image: The Infernal Blessing, or the Blessing Beneath Us

Let us now look at the blessings that are found in others and which lie outside of us. The first is found in those who are beneath us, that is, in the dead and the damned. Isn't it strange that some kind of a blessing can be found in them?

First, as we compare the lot of the damned with our own, we see how immeasurable our gain is. This may be gathered readily from the corresponding images of evils. Great as the evils of death and hell are that we see in the damned, so great certainly are the gains that we see in ourselves, and the greater our blessings, the worse are their evils. These matters commend to us the wonderful mercy of God. If we deem them lightly, we run the danger of being found ungrateful, of being condemned together with these men and of being even more cruelly tormented.

Because it is so common and so well known, this blessing probably affects us but little. Nevertheless, it is numbered among the highest blessings. A great portion of the Holy Scriptures speak of the wrath, the judgments, and the warnings of God. The examples of wretched men are especially effective when we enter into the feelings of those who endure such things and put ourselves in the place of these people. Then they will move and admonish us to praise the goodness of God who has preserved us from such evils.

Let us also compare them with God Himself, so that we may see the divine justice in their case. Since God is a just Judge, we must love and laud His justice and rejoice in God even when He miserably destroys the wicked in body and soul. Thus even hell is no less full of good, the supreme good, than is heaven. The justice of God is God Himself and God is the highest good. Therefore, even as His mercy, so must His justice or judgment be loved, praised, and glorified above all things.

The voice of praise and joy resounds throughout the whole Psalter, for the Lord is the Judge of the widow and the fatherless; He will be the defense of the poor and the Protector of the helpless and the enemy shall be confounded and the ungodly destroyed. (See Ps. 10:14; 68:5; 140:12.) If anyone in foolish pity should feel compassion for that generation that kills the righteous or for the crowd of wicked men, he will be found to be rejoicing in their iniquity and approving their actions. He deserves to perish in a manner like those whose sins he would condone.

Therefore, in this image we ought to rejoice in the godliness of all the saints and in the justice of God who very justly punishes the persecutors and thereby delivers His elect out of their hands. Therefore, just as you ought to consent with joy to the justice of God raging against your own sins, so you should approve of the justice which rages against the sinner, the enemy of all men and of God.

The Fifth Image: The Blessing on Our Left Hand

Having discussed those adversaries who are already damned, we now discuss those who are still in this life.

We find in them a twofold blessing. The first is that they so abound in temporal goods that the prophets are almost moved to envy. We read in Psalm 73:2-3, "But as for me, my feet almost stumbled, my steps had almost slipped, for I was envious of the unjust ones when I saw the peace which the sinners had." Later on he says, "Behold these are the sinners who prosper in the world and increase in riches." (v. 12)

Why else does God lavish so many blessings on them except to comfort us thereby and to show how gracious He is to those who are "pure in heart"? If He is good to the wicked, how much more will He be good to those who are good! While He does not vex the wicked with evil, He certainly does test the good with many evils so that they may acknowledge His goodness to them, not only in the blessings of the present, but even in those that are hidden and still to come.

Thus the visible blessings of the wicked are an incentive to us to hope for the blessings that are invisible and to disdain the evils that we suffer. In Matthew 6:26-30 Christ bids us to look at the birds of the air and the lilies of the field, saying, "If God, therefore, so clothes the grass which today is and tomorrow is cast into the oven, will He not much more clothe you, O men of little faith?" Hence, by comparing the blessings in which the wicked abound with the evils which we suffer, our faith is exercised and we receive God's consolation.

The other blessing, even more marvelous, is that in the providence of God the evils of our adversaries become blessings to us. Though their sins are a stumbling block to the weak, to the strong they are an exercise of their virtue, an opportunity for conflict, and the amassing of greater merit. "Blessed is the man who endures trials, for when he has stood the test he shall receive the crown of life" (James 1:12). What greater trial can there be than the host of evil examples?

Thus it is good for us always to be oppressed with some trouble, lest in our weakness we succumb to the offenses of the world and fall into sin. It is necessary for such offenses to come to furnish us with struggle and victory. But woe to the world because of its offenses (Matt. 18:7). But if God procures such great blessings for us in the sins of others, ought we not in our hearts believe that He will work much greater blessings for us in our own troubles, even though our flesh and blood judge it to be otherwise!

Even as God enables us to find our blessings in the sins of the world, so also are its persecutions intended to increase our blessings so that they may not be fruitless or in vain. The very things that work us harm are turned to our profit. All of Scripture, the writings of the Fathers, and the lives and deeds of the saints agree that those who inflict the greatest harm on the believers are their greatest benefactors, as long as they bear their sufferings in the right spirit. Thus if we are wise, we find ourselves dwelling in the midst of blessings, and yet, at the same time, in the midst of evils. All things are so wondrously tempered under the providence of God's goodness!

The Sixth Image: The Blessings on Our Right Hand

This is the church of the saints, the new creation of God, our brothers and our friends, in whom we see nothing but blessing, nothing but consolation, though not always with the eyes of the flesh, but with the eyes of the spirit. Nevertheless we must not disregard even these visible blessings of theirs, but rather learn that God wants to comfort us with them.

The Apostle instructs Timothy to admonish the rich of this world not to be haughty, but he does not forbid them to be rich (1 Tim. 6:17). The Scriptures remind us that Abraham, Isaac, and Jacob were rich men. Daniel and his companions held places of honor even in Babylon (Dan. 2:48-49). Moreover, many kings of Judah were saintly men. It is with reference to them that the psalmist says, "If I had said this, I would have rejected the generation of your children" (Ps. 73:15).

God gives an abundance of such blessings even to His people to comfort them and others. Still, these things are not their true blessings, but only shadows and signs of their real blessings, which are faith, hope, love, and other gifts and graces, which are shared with all through love.

This is the communion of saints in which we glory. Whose heart will not be lifted up when he believes that the blessings of all the saints are his blessings and his evil also theirs? That is the pleasant picture the Apostle paints in Galatians 6:2, "Bear one another's burdens and so fulfill the law of Christ." Therefore, when I suffer, I do not suffer alone, but Christ and all Christians suffer with me. "He who touches you touches the apple of My eye" (Zech. 2:8).

Consequently, I can actually glory in the blessings of others as though they were my very own. They are truly mine when I am grateful and joyful with the others. It may be that I am base and ugly, while those whom I love and admire are fair and beautiful. By my love I make not only their blessings but their very selves my own. By their honor my shame is now made honorable, my want is supplied by their abundance, and my sins are healed by their merits.

Who could then despair in his sins? Who would not rejoice in his sorrows? He no longer bears his sins and punishment alone, but is supported by so many holy children of God—yes, by Christ Himself. So great is the communion of saints in the church of Christ.

If a person does not believe this, he is an infidel and has denied Christ and the church. We are one body. Whatever another suffers, I also suffer and endure. Whatever good befalls him, befalls me. Thus Christ says that whatever is done unto one of the least of His brethren is done unto Him (Matt. 25:40). When a man receives only the smallest morsel of the bread in the sacrament, is he not said to partake of the bread? And if he despises one crumb of the bread, is he not said to have despised the bread?

Therefore, when we feel pain, when we suffer, when we die, let us believe firmly that it is not we alone, but Christ and the church who are in pain and are suffering and dying with us. Christ does not want us to be alone on the road of death, from which all men shrink. Indeed, we set out upon the road of suffering and death accompanied by the entire church. Actually, the church bears it more bravely than we do.

All that remains for us now is to pray that our eyes of faith may be opened to see the church around us. Then there will be nothing for us to fear, as is stated in Psalm 125:2, "As mountains are round about Jerusalem, so the Lord is round about His people, from this time forth and forever." Amen.

The Seventh Image: The Supernal Blessing, or the Blessing Above Us

The seventh image is Jesus Christ, the King of glory, rising from the dead. Here the heart can find its supreme joy and lasting possessions. Here there is not the slightest trace of evil, for "Christ being risen from the dead will not die again. Death no longer has dominion over Him" (Rom. 6:9). Here is that furnace of love and the fire of God in Zion, as Isaiah says, for Christ is not only born to us, but also given to us (Isa. 9:6). Therefore, His resurrection and everything that He accomplished through it are mine.

What is it that He has wrought by His resurrection? He has destroyed sin and raised up righteousness, abolished death and restored life, conquered hell and bestowed everlasting glory on us. These blessings are so incalculable that the mind of man hardly dares believe that they have been granted to us.

Thus the Christian may glory in the merits of Christ and in all His blessings as though he himself had won them. So truly are they his own that he can boldly dare to look forward to the judgment of God. Such a great thing is faith, such blessings does it bring us, such glorious sons of God does it make us! We cannot be sons without also inheriting our Father's blessings. Let Christians thus say in full confidence, "O death, where is your victory? O death, where is your sting? The sting of death is sin, and the strength of sin is the law. But thanks be to God who gave us the victory through Jesus Christ, our Lord" (1 Cor. 15:55-57). The law makes us sinners and sin makes us guilty of death. Who has conquered these two? It was Jesus Christ, rising from death, condemning sin and death, imparting His righteousness to us, bestowing His merits on us, and holding His hand over us. Now all is well with us; we fulfill the law and vanquish sin and death. For all this let there be honor, praise, and thanksgiving to God for ever and ever. Amen.

This, then, is the most sublime image, for in it we are

lifted up not only above our evils, but even above our blessings, and we are set down in the midst of strange blessings fathered by the labors of another. As it is impossible for Christ with His righteousness not to please God, so it is impossible for us, with our faith clinging to His righteousness, not to please Him. It is in this way that a Christian becomes almighty lord of all, having all things and doing all things. It is on this that our faith relies. He who does not believe this is like a deaf man hearing a story.

Part IV

Sayings in Which Luther Found Comfort

There are times when, for the sake of God's word, we must endure the hardship, anguish, and persecution which the holy Cross brings upon us. In such times we can rightfully bestir and strengthen ourselves with God's help in such a way that we can be bold, alert, and cheerful, committing our cause to God's gracious and fatherly will. Thus St. Paul says in 2 Timothy 3:12, "All who desire to live a godly life in Jesus Christ will be persecuted," and in Acts 14:22, "Through many tribulations we must enter into the kingdom of God."

1

Our cause rests in the hand of Him who distinctly tells us, "No one can snatch them out of My hand" (John 10:28). Furthermore, "the gates of hell shall not prevail against My church" (Matt. 16:18). And in Isaiah 46:4, "Even to your old age and to gray hairs I will bear you. I will carry and will save."

2

It would neither be good nor prudent to take matters into our own hands because we could and would easily be defeated.

3

In any case, it is true that God gave up His own Son for us all (Rom. 8:32). If that be true, why do we falter, or worry, or hang our heads? If God gave up His own Son for us all, how could He ever intend to forsake us in less important things?

4

Truly God is very much stronger and more powerful than the devil, as 1 John 4:4 says, "He who is in you is greater than he who is in the world."

5

If we perish then Christ the Almighty Ruler of the world Himself must suffer with us. Even if this cause[1] were to collapse, I would much rather be ruined with Christ than rule with Caesar.

6

Furthermore, this cause does not depend just on us, but there are many devout Christian people in other lands who make common cause with us and uphold us with heartfelt sighs and Christian prayer.

7

We possess God's many encouraging promises and rich assurances. In fact the entire psalter, all the Gospels—yes, all Scripture is filled with them and they are by no means to be scorned but should be highly valued, such as Psalm 55:22, "Cast your burden on the Lord and He will sustain you; He will never permit the righteous to be moved." And Psalm 27:14, "Wait for the Lord, be of good cheer; do not despair and wait

---

[1] i.e., the Reformation.

for the Lord!" Furthermore Christ Himself says in John 16:33, "Be of good cheer; I have overcome the world."

This cannot be wrong—I'm sure of it—that Christ, the Son of God, has overcome the world. Why do we tremble before the world as before a triumphant conqueror?

8

Though our faith is weak, let us pray earnestly along with the apostles (Luke 17:5), "Lord, increase our faith," and with the child's father (Mark 9:24), "Lord, I believe: help my unbelief!"

9

The cause of Christ was in greater peril in the times of the Roman emperors Diocletian, Maximinius, and others who persecuted the Christian church in horrible ways and attempted to destroy it completely, and likewise in the times of John Huss and others, than it is in our own times.

10

Though the cause be great, He who has brought it about, who directs and guides it, is great too, yes, the Almighty Creator of heaven and earth. This is by no means our cause, so why should we keep on tormenting ourselves over it or plaguing ourselves to death?

11

If this cause, this doctrine, be a mistaken one, why do we not recant? But if it be a righteous cause—and as true as God lives and will remain in eternity, it is such—why do we make lies out of God's many comforting, unchanging, and eternal promises? He bids us be of good cheer and joyful (Ps. 32:11), "Be glad in the Lord," and "The Lord is near to all who call upon Him, to all who call upon Him in truth. He fulfills the desire of all who fear Him. He hears their cry, and saves them" (Ps. 145:18-19). And "Because he cleaves to Me, I will deliver him; I will protect him, because he knows My name. I will be with him in trouble, I will rescue him and honor him. With long life will I satisfy him and show him My salvation" (Ps. 91:14-16).

12

Even though we worry and fret so much, such needless anxiety will avail us nothing. We only plague and trouble ourselves and make matters all the worse. God wants us to look to Him as our God and Father in Christ, to call upon Him in every time of need and to be confident that He will provide for us; as St. Peter says, quoting Psalm 55:22, "Cast all your anxieties on Him for He cares about you" (1 Peter 5:7), and as Christ Himself says (Matt. 6:31), "You should not be anxious."

13

The devil and his cohorts can do no worse than slay us bodily. They cannot touch our souls at all, as Christ says when He comforted His own (Matt. 10:28), "Do not fear those who kill the body but cannot kill the soul."

14

Christ, our dear Lord and Saviour, died once for our sin, as it is written in Romans 4:25 and 6:10, Hebrews 5:3 and 9:28. Henceforth He will not die again for the sake of righteousness and truth, but rules as all-powerful Lord over every creature. If this be true, as Scripture continually testifies, what are we afraid of?

15

Though, if God so ordains, we ourselves might be destroyed for the sake of His Word, the Almighty and Merciful God who in Christ has become our Father, will then be a kind and gracious Father and Guardian, Defender and Protector for our wives and children, our widows and orphans, and He will manage matters a thousand times better than we could if we were living with them.

16

Our forefathers and ancestors did not have this glorious, noble, precious treasure, namely, the true and pure understanding of the divine Word which, God be praised, we now have in ample measure. Nor did they experience these days which have brought the Word to light again, just before Judgment Day. This indescribable blessing has been bestowed upon us as a gift of God's kindness and grace. This very same God will continue to be God and Creator after we are gone, as He has been before us, and to the end of the world He will always gather to Himself a little flock and uphold it. He will not die with us nor cease to exist, as we of little faith imagine.

17

The First Commandment places our children and descendants under God's protection and providence, as God Himself says, "I show mercy to thousands of those who love Me and keep My commandments" (Ex. 20:6). We ought rightfully to believe these exalted and comforting words of the Divine Majesty.

Though our faith be weak, we nevertheless rely on God's honor that He can and will do what He says and promises.

18

Let us be calmly confident in this cause which has to do with God's Word. Christ, whose cause it is, will staunchly defend and uphold it against the cunning of the vile devil and the tyranny of the wicked and deceitful world. For those who confess Him before this evil and adulterous generation and must suffer much thereby, Christ in turn will confess them before His heavenly Father and requite them for their suffering with the delights of eternity (Matt. 10:32). God Himself says (1 Sam. 2:30), "He who honors Me, I will honor." Even if the waves of the sea are strong and huge billows rise up and roar furiously as though they would drown us, the Lord is still on high and has begun a kingdom as wide as the world which He now rules and has decreed that it shall endure. He is greater, yes, almighty, and He will accomplish it. Amen.

There is no other way—if we desire to possess Christ, to live and to rule with Him in eternity, then suffering must first be endured.

Because this is so, why should we heed the rage and fury of such deadly powers, of whom Psalm 2:4 says that God in heaven laughs at them and holds them in derision.

If the eternal and omnipotent Emperor whose name is God, and who lives to all eternity, mocks and derides them, why should we fear them, or mourn and weep? Truly, God does not mock them in His own defense. He will always be the One dwelling in heaven, no matter how they rage against Him. But He mocks them to encourage us, so that we may take heart and bravely laugh at their onslaughts.

Therefore the only thing necessary for us to do is to believe and to pray most confidently in Christ's name that God will give us strength, since He has erected His kingdom and this is His doing. It is He who without our help, counsel, thought, or effort has brought His kingdom forth and has advanced and preserved it to this day. I have no doubt that He will consummate it without our advice or assistance. Because "I know in whom I believe," as St. Paul says (2 Tim. 1:12), I am certain that He will grant me more, do far more abundantly, and help and counsel us beyond all that we ask or think (Eph. 3:20). He is called the Lord who can and will help in a wonderful, glorious, and mighty way, particularly when the need is the greatest. We are meant to be human beings, not divine. So let us take comfort in His Word and, trusting His promise, call upon Him confidently for deliverance in time of distress and He will help.

That is all there is to it; we have no alternative; otherwise, eternal unrest would be our reward. May God save us from that for the sake of His dear Son, our Saviour and eternal Priest, Jesus Christ. Amen.

Part V

Sermons

Sermon: The Golden Rule

This is one of Luther's first sermons. One has said, "It is the most penetrating sermon on law and judgment which we have from the young Luther."

Mathew 7:12, "Whatever you wish that men would do to you, do so to them; for this is the law and the prophets."

First, it should be noted that human goods are of three kinds. The first are external, such as silver, gold, clothing, land, houses, servants, wines, children, oxen, etc. These are called external goods because they lie outside of human nature. Secondly, there are the physical and personal goods, such as health, strength, beauty, aptitude of the senses, and reputation and honor. Thirdly, there are spiritual or internal goods, such as knowledge, virtue, love, faith. These are called internal and spiritual because they lie solely in the mind and spirit. And the external goods are symbols of these internal and spiritual goods.

With these goods, then, each person can conduct himself towards his neighbor in two ways. First, with them he can do harm and evil to him, or, second, he can advance and benefit him. An example of the first is when one steals external goods or destroys the health of the body with blows and poison or takes from him his internal goods, such as knowledge, by seducing him into error, or virtue, by inciting him to evil. An example of the second way is when one gives him food and clothing or heals his infirmities or protects his body or teaches him something better and incites him to do good. Therefore we have in Scripture two rules to guide us in the use of these goods: Psalms 33 and 37:27, "defeat from evil," with respect to the first and "do good," with respect to the second way.

It is not sufficient for salvation that a man merely refrain from doing harm to his neighbor with these goods. It is required rather that he be useful to him and benefit him. This doctrine is proved by reason, authority, and analogy.

First, by *reason*. If merely refraining from doing harm were sufficient for salvation, then much wood in the forest and many stones in the depths of the ocean would be saved, for they obviously do no harm or evil to anyone through these goods. But this is not true. Thus the one who merely does no harm would be like wood and stones, and this is not sufficient for salvation.

Second, by *authority* of Scripture. Our text says, "Whatever you wish that men would do to you." It does not say: whatever harm you wish that men should not do to you, do not this harm to them. This is true, of course, and necessary, but it is not sufficient; we must also do good to the other person.

The rich reveller of the parable (Luke 16:19-31) was not damned because he robbed or did evil with respect to his goods, for he feasted and clothed himself sumptuously every day. He was damned rather because he did not do good to his neighbor, Lazarus.

In the parable of the slothful servant (Matt. 25:14-30) who received the one talent and hid it in the ground, condemnation came not because he took something away from others, but because he did not give to others. So it will be with us. To us has been given as a talent what we are able to do. All that we are capable of we have not of ourselves, but from God. And in all this we are required to do to our neighbor what we are able to do.

Sins of Omission

The judgment of the Lord will not speak of whether one has harmed or done evil with his goods, but rather that he has not done good. Therefore, Christ says (Matt. 25:42), "I was hungry and you gave Me no food, I was thirsty and you gave Me no drink . . ." He does not say: I had food and you stole it from Me . . . but rather, "You gave Me no food, no drink." Similarly, He says, "I was a stranger and you did not welcome Me, naked and you did not clothe Me, sick . . . and you did not visit Me."

Third, it is also proved by *analogy:* wild beasts and irrational animals keep this law. When a pig is slaughtered or captured and other pigs see this, we observe that the other pigs clamor or grunt as if in compassion. Chickens and geese and all wild animals do the same thing. Only a man, who is rational, does not spring to the aid of his suffering neighbor in time of need. Man kills, robs, wounds, defames, seduces, and makes sad. Beyond this, he is also capable of cherishing hatred and jealousy.

From this it is possible to draw several lessons and conclusions.

First, he who sees a naked man and does not clothe him, if he is able, will not be saved. For if he were naked, he would certainly wish to be clothed by one who was able to do so.

Second, he who sees a thirsty or hungry man and does not feed him, if he is able, will be damned, for he acts against the law and the prophets.

Third, he who sees another person sinning or erring . . . and does not instruct and rebuke and admonish him, but rather laughs and applauds, that person sins the same sin.

Fourth, if those who merely do not good to their neighbor commit sin and are damned, where will they be who actually do evil and harm to others? Therefore, let each one place this example of the Lord before his eyes like a mirror and note it well, for it is good and He would have it to be the whole law and the prophets.

It is possible that one may think to himself, would it not be sufficient if I wish the other person well in my heart? Or, I will let him go in peace, disengage myself from him, and do neither good nor evil to him. Or, is not what I have my own? I can do with it what I will.

The answer to the first question is, would you be content with merely good will on the part of another if you were injured or offended by him? The answer to the second suggestion is that one cannot always know the reason why the offended one does not do good to the offender, whether the motive is love of revenge or love of justice or fear of danger. Therefore, this is best: hold up the mirror of these words to your conscience and see whether any such motive would prompt you not to wish any good to be done to you by others if they cherished any such motive toward you. Then you are saved. Otherwise, beware. To the third question, one may reply that all the goods we have are from God and are not given to us to retain and abuse, but rather to dispense.

In conclusion, every person should remember that we cannot help ourselves; only God can. Our works are utterly worthless. So shall we have the peace of God. And every person should so perform his work that it benefits not only himself alone, but also his neighbor. If he is rich, his wealth should benefit the poor. If he is poor, his service should benefit the rich. Thus, no one's work should benefit him alone.

Therefore, dear friends, remember that God has risen up for our sakes. Let us also arise to be helpful to the weak in faith, and so direct our work that God may be pleased with it. So shall we receive the peace He has given to us today. Amen.

The first sermon preached at the castle in Weimar, October 19, 1522. Sets forth the essence of the Christian faith simply, clearly, vividly, and practically.

Matthew 22:37-39, "You shall love . . . God with all your heart, and with all your soul, and with all your mind . . . and your neighbor as yourself, etc."

The Gospel consists of two questions: First, what is the greatest commandment by which one is saved? and second, what does the law require? And these two must agree with each other.

It is the commandment of Christ that one must love Him with the whole soul, the whole mind, and all powers, and the neighbor as one's self; and he who has this has everything and God dwells in him. But you say: Oh, it is utterly impossible for one to keep these two commandments. Yes, it is impossible for you to keep or perform them. God must do it in you; for Him it is possible.

The law requires that we love God with all our powers, etc., and our neighbor as ourselves. Now if it is true that the law requires us to love God and our neighbor with all our soul and all our powers, then it is certain that one is not rightly fasting, praying, crying to God, and doing other things if he does not first love God and his neighbor. If the works are not done out of love, then they are absolutely nothing and there is nothing good in this love.

Circumcision among the Jews was commanded by God. They were obliged to do it to show that they loved God.

Abraham sacrificed his son because this is what God wanted (Gen. 22:1-19). According to nature it was a foolish, stupid command. But Abraham was willing to follow God, and because of the love he bore for God, it was pleasing to God. But God does not care about his killing; he was looking at his love and obedience.

We read that as the disciples were going through the grainfields they plucked ears of grain and ate them (Matt. 12:1-8). The Jews were angry over this, but Christ said, "Your sabbath is no commandment to Me; I don't care about that." The point is that the disciples were hungry and, having loved Christ and followed Him, they preferred to break the sabbath rather than leave Him. The Jews did not see the love.

Love Embraces All Commandments

Thus, all the commandments of the law depend on love. That is to say, if they are not done out of love, they are contrary to God and are nothing. It is not to be done for the sake of other works, for your eye should be kept only on the work of love. Christ imputes everything to love and our whole life should consist in this.

But isn't it pitiful that a priest has a commandment, not from God, but from the pope, to pray seven hours, to fast the long fasts, and to do other things. More importance is attached to obeying the pope than to do for the love of Christ. When a lay person is commanded as a penance to go to Rome or make a pilgrimage to this or that saint and is to go barefoot, and he sees his neighbor suffering want and the poor man asks for help, he should look to the love of Christ and help the man and let the pilgrimage go. For love of one's neighbor is like the first commandment.

But nowadays when a pilgrimage is imposed upon a person and his brother and neighbor ask him for help, he goes to confession and receives the penance that he should help his neighbor and that he is unable to perform the pope's commandment. Thus he has more regard for the pope's commandment than for Christ's.

We have had blind preachers for a long time. They have been totally blind themselves and leaders of the blind, as the Gospel says. They have left the Gospel and followed their own ideas and preferred the work of men to the work of God. (See Mark 7:8-9.)

What is meant by "with all your heart"? Nothing but that I do willingly and gladly everything that my God commands me. Loving with one's "whole soul" is also to love with one's whole, inmost spirit, and one's whole life. Where do you find that kind of a person? Man, whether he hears, sees, wakes, sleeps, walks or stands still, wants always to live his life without being bothered at all. That person who loves best is one who loves with his own soul.

Loving "with all your mind" is to surrender oneself to God with one's whole mind so that even His commands become good and right. But in these days our minds have been utterly corrupted by man-made laws, for the evil spirit usually concentrates on seizing the human mind and spirit.

This, then, is the love which Christ would have. And here we find that we are all under condemnation; no one does or has this law. When this law is kept, one needs no other law.

Sermon on Cross and Suffering, April 16, 1530, a Harmony of Matthew 27, Luke 24, and John 19

Since there are many false fanatics abroad who accuse us of teaching nothing but faith alone and leaving out the doctrine of good works and the holy cross and suffering, we shall at this time speak of the Passion, the kind of cross we bear and suffer, and how we should bear and suffer it.

We note in the first place not only that Christ by His suffering saved us from the devil, death, and sin, but also that His suffering is an example we are to follow in our suffering. God has appointed that we should not only believe in the crucified Christ, but also be crucified with Him, as He clearly shows many places in the Gospels: "He who does not take his cross and follow Me is not worthy of Me" (Matt. 10:38).

Therefore each must bear a part of the holy cross. St. Paul says, "In my flesh I complete what is lacking in Christ's afflictions" (Col. 1:24). It is as if he were saying Christ's whole Christendom is not fully completed; we too must follow after in order that none of the suffering of Christ may be lacking or lost.

It should be, however, the kind of suffering that is worthy of the name—such as some great danger of property, honor, body, and life. It should not be the kind of suffering which we have chosen for ourselves, as the fanatics choose their suffering. It should be the kind of suffering which, if it were possible, we would gladly be rid of, suffering visited upon us by the devil or the world. And one must hold fast and submit to the knowledge that we must suffer to be conformed to Christ and that it cannot be otherwise. When one knows this, it is the more bearable.

This the fanatics, who select their own cross, cannot do; they resist it and fight against it. And yet they can reproach us, as if we did not teach aright concerning suffering. But our teaching is that none should dictate or choose his own cross and suffering, but rather, when it comes, patiently bear and suffer it. But they are wrong, not only with respect to their choosing their own cross, but also in that they flaunt their suffering and make a great merit of it and thus blaspheme God because it is not a true suffering.

Suffer Willingly

If you are willing to suffer, very well, then the treasure and consolation which is promised and given to you is so great that you ought to suffer willingly and joyfully because Christ and His suffering is being bestowed upon you and is made your own. If you can believe this, then in time of great fear and trouble you will be able to say: Even though I suffer long, what is that compared with the great treasure which God has given to me—that I shall live eternally with Him, both now and in the world to come?

Furthermore, every Christian should submit himself to this suffering, for he is sure that it will work for his good and that Christ, for His Word's sake, will not only help us to bear this suffering but also turn it to our advantage. St. Paul says (1 Cor. 10:13), "God is faithful, and He will not let you be tempted beyond your strength, but with the temptation will also provide the way of escape."

The cause of our suffering is the same as that for which all the saints have suffered from the beginning. Of course, the whole world must bear witness that we are not suffering because of public scandal or vice, such as adultery, fornication, murder, etc. Rather we suffer because we hold the Word of God, preach it, learn it, practice it. Since this is the cause of our suffering, we have the same promise and the same cause for suffering which all the saints have always had.

In our suffering we should so act that we give our greatest attention to the promise in order that our cross and affliction may be turned to good—to something we could never have asked for or thought. This is precisely the thing which makes a difference between the Christian's suffering and that of other men. Other people also have their afflictions, cross, and misfortune just as they also have their times when they can sit in the rose garden and employ their good fortune and goods as they please. But when they run into affliction and suffering, they do not have the mighty promises and confidence in God which Christians have. We see that they cannot endure even the small afflictions and when the strong afflictions occur, they despair altogether.

Look to the Word—in Suffering

This then is the true art, that in suffering and cross we should look to the Word, even as He said, "In Me you shall have peace, but in the world, tribulation" (John 16:33). It is as if He were saying: "Danger and terror will surely hit you if you accept My Word; but let it come; this will happen to you because of Me. So be of good cheer; I will not forsake you, I will be with you and help you no matter how great the affliction may be."

Therefore in affliction every Christian should so arm himself that he may defend and guard himself with the five, comfortable assurances which Christ, our Lord, has left us when we suffer for His Word's sake. But if we do not do this—if we let the comfortable sayings go, then when the cross comes, the same thing that happened to Eve in paradise will happen to us. She let the Word go and kept thinking what a fine apple it was and that, after all, such a little thing was of no great importance. So she went her way. And when one lets the Word go, there can be no other result.

You see that we teach these two things when we preach suffering and cross. And anybody who accuses us of teaching nothing about suffering is doing us an injustice. But we do not make our suffering meritorious before God. Christ alone did that, and to Him alone belongs the glory.

The Discipline of Suffering

We want also to consider why our Lord God sends us such suffering. The reason is that in this way He wants to make us conformed to the image of His dear Son, so that we may become like Him here in suffering and there, in that life to come, in honor and glory; as He says, "Was it not necessary that the Christ should suffer and enter into glory?" (Luke 24:26) God cannot accomplish this in us except through suffering and affliction.

Another reason that God sends us suffering is that although God does not want to assault and torment us, the devil does. He is by nature so malicious and venomous that he cannot endure anything that is good.

It irks him that an apple should be growing on a tree; it pains and vexes him that you have a sound finger, and if he were able he would tear everything apart and put it out of joint.

But there is nothing to which he is so hostile as the beloved Word, for only the Word exposes him and shows everybody how black he is. If our dear God were not guarding us by His angels and we were able to see the devil's cunning, conspiring, and lying, we should die of the sight of it alone, so many are the guns he has ranged against us.

So the two heroes meet, each doing as much as possible. The devil brews one calamity after another. He lashes out to see if he can smash the little vessel. Our Lord looks on for awhile and puts us in a tight place so that we may learn from experience that the small, weak, miserable Word is stronger than the devil and the gates of hell.

It is also necessary that we suffer, not only that God may prove His honor, power, and strength against the devil, but also in order that when we are not in trouble and suffering, this excellent treasure which we have may not make us sleepy and secure. God must discipline and drive us that our faith may grow stronger and bring the Saviour more deeply into our hearts, for just as we cannot get along without eating and drinking, so we cannot get along without affliction and suffering.

Finally, the Christian suffering is noble and precious above all other human suffering because, since Christ Himself suffered, He also hallowed the suffering of all His Christians. Are we not foolish people? We have run to Rome and other places to visit shrines; why do we not cherish the cross and suffering which touched Christ more closely than any garment did His body?

Through the suffering of Christ, the suffering of all His saints has become utterly holy, for it has been touched with Christ's suffering.

Since we know that it is God's pleasure that we should suffer and that God's glory is manifested in our suffering, why should we not be bold to suffer? It is a thousand times better to have suffered for the sake of Christ, who promised us comfort and help in suffering, than to suffer and despair and perish without comfort and help for the sake of the devil.

Sermon on the Sum of the Christian Life, preached on Worlitz, November 24, 1532

First Timothy 1:5-7: "The aim of our charge is love that issues from a pure heart and a good conscience and sincere faith. Certain persons by swerving from these have wandered away into vain discussion, desiring to be teachers of the law, without understanding either what they are saying or the things about which they make assertions." (Luther's translation)

Paul begins his epistle to his disciple Timothy by urging him to see to it that teachers do not arise who can blab a lot about the law and bring up many new questions of what one must do to be religious and to be praised as being more learned than others. Yet they never get to the point where they teach anything that is sure and right; they never get hold of the middle, the beginning, or the end of anything, but just go on talking about how to be religious, how to do good works, and the like. However, they themselves do not understand what this means.

But the right master, Paul says, would be the one who grasps the main point and can put his finger on the sum total—that is, the state of the heart and conscience and the whole man. What, then, is the sum total of what should be preached? Paul's answer is, "The aim of our charge is love that issues from a pure heart and a good conscience and sincere faith."

There you have everything in a nutshell, expressed in the finest and fullest way and yet briefly and quickly said and easily retained. You must have the love that flows from a pure heart and a good conscience and sincere faith. All right preaching starts from there and remains there.

Love in German means nothing else except "to be favorably and affectionately disposed toward a person from the heart and to show him all kindness and friendship." Now these other teachers also use this word. They preach and puff a lot about love. But they do so only from their own angle and turn it to their own advantage, just as the heretics, the godless, and the rascals also have love, but only among themselves while they hate and persecute all good Christians and would gladly murder them if they could.

God has commanded me to let my love go out to my neighbor and be kindly disposed to all, whether they be my friends or enemies, just as our heavenly Father does. He allows His sun to rise and shine on the good and evil and is most kind to those who are constantly dishonoring Him. Why? Out of sheer, pure love. This is a real, divine, total, and perfect love, which does not single out one person nor cut and divide itself, but goes out freely to all.

The other kind of love—when I am a good friend to one who can serve and help me and who esteems me and hate the one who is not on my side—is false love. For it does not issue from a heart which is basically good and pure, the same toward all alike, but which rather seeks only its own and is stuffed full of love for itself and not for others. If you praise and honor that kind of person, he smiles; but if you make a sour face at him or say something he doesn't like to hear, he flares up, begins to scold and curse, and the friendship is over.

On the contrary, he who has a pure heart should be so in accord with God's Word and His example, that he will wish everyone well and do good to all, as God wishes him well and gives His divine love to him. If God can bestow all good upon Judas the traitor or Caiaphas, as well as upon His good children, why should I not also do the same?

Yes, you may say, but he is my enemy and he does nothing but evil to me. Yes, he is God's enemy too and he does far more evil to Him than he can do to you or me. But my love shall not grow dim or cease because he is evil and unworthy of it. If he is evil, he will find it out, but his wickedness must not overcome me. On the contrary, if through love I can rebuke and admonish him or pray for him that he may amend his ways and escape punishment, this I should do gladly. But to want to fly at him and become his enemy and do evil to him besides I will not do, for what good will it do me? It will not make me any better and it certainly will make him worse.

Made Pure by the Word

But what is it that makes the heart pure? The answer is that there is no better way of making it pure than through the highest purity, which is God's Word. Get that into your heart and order your life by it, and your heart will become pure. For example, take this saying, "You shall love your neighbor as yourself" (Matt. 19:19), and order your life by that and you will see very well whether it will not wash it clean and scour out the selfishness which is there. For when He commands you to love your neighbor, He excludes nobody, be he friend or enemy, good or evil. If you look at him in the way the Word teaches and directs you, your heart will become pure and your love true so that you will make no false distinction between persons.

It is true that the good man is more likeable and everybody naturally is glad to associate with him, whereas one shies away from rough, evil people. But this is a derived or borrowed love which cleaves outwardly to the good it sees in a person and lasts no longer than this good lasts and can be enjoyed. But love should be a flowing love, which flows from the inside of the heart like a fresh stream that goes on flowing and cannot be stopped or dried up. This love says: 'I love you, not because you are good or bad, for I draw my love, not from your goodness, as from another's fountain, but from my own little spring, from the Word, which is grafted in my heart.' Then it flows out abundantly and is there for all who need it, touching both the good person and the bad, both friend and foe.

This is the way to preach if you want to teach rightly concerning love, which is required by the law and of which these others know nothing and for which they have no regard, even though they talk a lot about the law and dispute at length about love. They do not see that this is the way we must love—that it must flow outward from the inside—that a man must have a pure heart. They operate with nothing but rambling and useless ideas, with purely dead dreams.

You can see in every station of life how each person in his calling should do the work committed to him and practice the work of love. A servant, for example, may think no farther than this: my master gives me wages and that's why I serve him; otherwise I have no regard for him. He does not have a pure heart or intention, for he works only to obtain a bit of bread. When this ceases his service also ceases. But if he were a good Christian, he would say: I'm not going to work because my master pays me or does not pay me, or because he is good or bad, but rather because the Word of God tells me: "Servants, be obedient to your masters, as to Christ" (Eph. 6:5). Then it issues of itself from the heart and he will say: I will serve my master and take my wages, but the chief reason I do so is that I shall be serving my Lord who has commanded me to do this and I know this is well pleasing to Him.

Or take a lord or prince who must govern. He may reason: God has committed the government to me that I should rule. But if I am concerned only to hold on to my dignity, riches, and power, then my heart is not pure, even though I do the work of a prince in such a way that the world cannot complain nor the emperor or the lawyers criticize or rebuke me according to their laws.

In the sight of God, his heart is impure. The work of no man pleases God if the Word of God is not in it.

You see, then, that the Word is the cause, foundation, ground, fountain, and spring of love from the heart and all good works, if they are to please God, cannot do so unless the heart first is pure. That is why He causes His Word to be preached—in order that we conform ourselves to it in all our life and action. Let us allow nothing to hinder or trouble us or make us weak or weary, even though we suffer loss, ingratitude, and contempt because of it. Let us say: I did not begin this for man's sake and therefore I will not cease because of men. I shall do it for God's sake, let happen what may.

A Good Conscience

Now, concerning a *good conscience*. Love should issue from a heart which has a joyful, quiet conscience both toward men and God. Toward men in the sense in which Paul boasted that he had so lived that he had neither offended nor grieved anybody nor given a bad example. Moses too gloried in such a conscience against his rebellious people (Num. 16:15).

This is the kind of glory and confidence every Christian should possess that he may so live before every man that none may bring any complaint against him to terrify and dismay his conscience. This is what it means to have a good conscience toward men.

Even though such a conscience will not be able to stand before God's judgment, any more than the purity of heart which consists in outward life and works of love can stand before Him, nevertheless we should have this kind of a heart in order that we may comfort ourselves before Him and say: This God has enjoined and commanded; therefore I do it out of a pure heart and good conscience, and I would not willingly do otherwise nor offend and hurt anybody. For anyone who does not pay attention to living his life in such a way that he can put everyone to silence and prove before men that he has lived, spoken, and done well, that man is not yet a Christian and has neither a pure heart nor love within him. For if a person is inclined to rely on the doctrine of faith as if he can do whatever he likes whether it harms or helps his neighbors, this will do him no good. Otherwise this doctrine will get the reputation of giving license to every kind of excess and villainy.

In order that all this may be acceptable before God, there is one other thing that must be added, *sincere faith*. There is no man on earth who can say: I know I have done everything and before God I owe nothing. Even the holiest of saints must confess: I have done what I could, perhaps, but I have failed far oftener than I know.

Here the chief article of our doctrine must come to our help, namely that our Lord Jesus Christ who came into the world, and suffered and died for us, now sits at the right hand of the Father pleading our cause as our Saviour. Through Him we may say before God: Although I am not pure and cannot have a good conscience, yet I cleave to Him who possesses perfect purity and good conscience and offers them for me, indeed, gives them to me.

This, then, is the faith which is neither feigned nor hypocritical. Before the judgment seat of the world I am content to be dealt with according to the law; then I will answer and do what I ought. But before Thee I would appeal to no law, but rather flee to the Cross and plead for grace and accept it as I am able.

The Law and the Gospel

We must now learn to distinguish between the two parts which are called the Law and the Gospel. The Law brings us before the judgment seat, for it demands that we must be good and love out of a pure heart and a good conscience. Its purpose is to make us exercise ourselves in this. But when it demands that you settle accounts and pay what it requires, there it cancels itself; for even if you have performed what it requires, this still will not stand before God, since before Him there will still be much which is lacking which you have not done and which you do not even realize you have not done. Then you must simply despair and there is no help or counsel for you unless you know that you can flee from the judgment seat to the mercy seat.

Thus through faith we are made wholly safe and secure, so that we shall not be condemned, not because of our holiness or purity, but because of Christ, because through this faith we cleave to Him as our mercy seat—sure that in Him no wrath can remain, but only love, pardon, and forgiveness. Thus the heart is made pure and the conscience secure before God.

Here we must see to it that our faith is not false, or, as Paul says, feigned, but rather sincere, for if faith fails or proves to be false, then everything fails. There have always been many, as there still are, who talk a lot about faith and pretend to be masters not only of the Law but also of the Gospel, and say as we do: Faith is what does it. However, then they go on to say that the Law and good works must be added to it, otherwise faith does not avail. This is not to teach faith purely and sincerely. If faith is to be unalloyed and unfeigned, Christ and my works must be rightly distinguished.

The man who can do this will be the justified man; all others operate with a feigned faith. They talk a lot about faith, but they mix things together, as a barkeeper mixes water and wine. Therefore, keep these two widely separated from each other, so that neither can approach the other: on one side your life and holiness and the judgment seat, which demands and drives you to have a good conscience and live rightly before men, but on the other side your sin before the mercy seat where God will lovingly welcome you and take you into His arms like a beloved child with all your sins and frightened conscience and will no more remember any wrath.

If faith were preached that way, men would be justified and all the rest. A pure heart and good conscience through genuine, perfect love would follow, for the man who through faith is sure in his heart that he has a gracious God who is not angry with him, though he deserves wrath, that man goes out and does everything joyfully. Toward God, therefore, he stands in a relationship of certainty that he is secure for Christ the Mediator's sake.

This way is difficult to learn, especially for us who have been so trained in the doctrine of works and pointed only to the Law and ourselves. And besides this add our own nature, which is itself inclined in this direction. It is thus so rooted and strengthened by habit that we cannot get away from it. Thus we must contend both with our nature and with habit. It will be exceedingly difficult to get into another habit of thinking in which we clearly separate faith and love, for the muck still clings to us. We even want to haggle with God to make Him regard our life and for our sake turn His judgment seat into a mercy seat. But it cannot be done.

Let anybody try this and he will see how hard and bitter a thing it is for a man who all his life has been mired in his work of righteousness to pull himself out of it. I myself have now been preaching and cultivating it through reading and writing for almost twenty years and still I feel the old clinging dirt of wanting to deal so with God that I may contribute something so that He will have to give me His grace in exchange for my holiness. Still I cannot get it into my head that I should surrender myself completely to sheer grace. It is no wonder that others find it hard to grasp faith thus purely, especially when the situation is made worse by the devil's preachers who emphasize the Law by quoting such texts as, "Do this and you will live" (Luke 10:28) and "If you would enter life, keep the commandments" (Matt. 19:17).

Therefore let us hold fast to this text, for it is

excellently expressed and a pure, perfect teaching of how we are to be righteous before God and men and how a pure heart, a good conscience, and sincere faith are to be brought together so that out of them all our life should flow and continue. Then we shall have found and fulfilled the meaning of the Law. But above all, it teaches us that we must look to Christ and bring Him into it, who "is the end of the law" (Rom. 10:4).

"I heard the timer go off in the kitchen," Frances said. She grabbed Dottie's elbow and bustled off. Following Frances's lead, perhaps understanding his and Dixie's need for privacy, Bubba and Chad announced that it was time to leave.

"We've promised to help Milo move furniture into his new double-wide this evening," Chad said. "He's got some girl-friend from up north who needs a place to stay. Says she's sick with a cold and has a little dog."

Dixie and Kyle shared a baffled glance, but it went unobserved by Bubba and Chad, who ducked into the kitchen to say goodbye to Frances and Dottie.

As the two men walked out the door, Kyle was gazing at Dixie, could hardly take his eyes off her. He was glad to be blessedly alone with the woman he loved.

"I have to tell you something," he said. "I was afraid you'd been in an accident and I panicked. I was terrified that you'd been hurt or worse before I could tell you all that's in my heart. Oh, Dixie, when I saw your car parked here at this house, I felt as if I'd been given a second chance, and I couldn't mess it up. That's why I didn't wait for a more romantic moment to ask you to marry me. If you like, we can do this over with a bouquet of flowers, a ring and beautiful music under the moon somewhere. I'll even get down on bended knee. When I saw you, realized that you were all right, my shattered world came back together again."

"Wait," Dixie said. "Why did you think I'd been in an accident?"

He told her about the radio bulletin, the detour and the car that so resembled hers. Her eyes grew round, and she rested her cheek against his shoulder for a moment.

"Dixie, why are you here? Is this some family occasion?"

She led him to the couch and they sat down as she started to explain. "Memaw invited us to stay here until Andrea leaves, and I took her up on it. I told Andrea to tell you, but you haven't seen her. Then Bubba and Chad stopped by because they saw my car parked outside and they wanted to say hi."

"Right."

"The surprising thing is, Kyle, that when I got here, Memaw shared a confidence that blows my mind."

"Which is?" He couldn't stop looking at her, couldn't believe how lucky he was to be the man she loved.

Dixie paused for dramatic effect. "Kyle, Memaw drank moonshine and slept with Granddaddy before she was married. Back in those days, that was an unconventional thing to do."

After taking a moment to absorb this astonishing information, Kyle threw his head back and laughed. "Your grandmother is my kind of girl."

"She doesn't mind if we share a bed at her house after all. It's amazing."

He kissed her forehead. "*You're* amazing. I'm glad I found you."

"So am I. Oh, bad news. Lana isn't going to buy the house."

Closing this deal had meant so much to her. "I'm sorry, Dixie."

She brightened. "Yes, but the day hasn't been a total waste. From my point of view, I mean."

"Promise me we'll never part in the morning without our goodbye kiss," he said.

"That's easy. I was out of sorts all day because we started out on a sour note. We won't do that anymore, Kyle."

"When can we get married?" He'd say the vows tomorrow if they could arrange it.

"We could have a big June wedding in church with bridesmaids and flower girls and a reception at the Moose Hall. I'll borrow Memaw's string of pearls. Oh, and the blue garter that my sister wore at her wedding. I'll wear a long white dress with lots of buttons down the back, a demi-train and—"

"And a real low neckline?" he asked optimistically, figuring that if she was going to insist on a wedding with all the trimmings, there should be something for him to look forward to.

"Maybe. Voncille's daughters can be flower girls, and little Petey can be the ring bearer, and we'll need to find something for Paul to do so he doesn't get bored. Maybe he could recite a poem or something. And—"

"Dixie, honey, slow down. Shouldn't we figure out more practical things first, such as who takes out the garbage?"

"I'm more interested in a band for the reception. There's this group out of Florence—"

He stopped her in midsentence by kissing her. "Let's talk about that later."

She sighed. "Okay. I'm just so happy and I love you so much and I never want to be apart as long as we live."

"That's more or less the whole idea of marriage," he said drily and was rewarded by an incandescent smile.

"Hey, bride-to-be," he said softly, tipping her face toward his. "There's one thing I want to settle right now."

"What's that, future husband?" She had tears in her eyes as she spoke, but they were tears for happy, not for sad.

"Have you ever made love on your honeymoon before?"

"No," she said seriously, "but I'm pretty sure you and I can figure it out just fine."

Ms. Dixie Lee Smith

and

Mr. Kyle Tecumseh Sherman

have chosen the first day

of their new life together

as June 14 2008.

You are invited to share in their joy

as they exchange marriage vows

at 7:00 p.m.

Sycamore Branch Community Church

Yewville, South Carolina.

Reception immediately following at the

Loyal Order of the Moose Hall

2129 Palmetto Street

Yewville

Y'all come!

DIXIE'S CARAWAY-SEED CAKE

2 sticks margarine
3 cups sugar
1 stick butter
6 eggs
3 cups plain flour
1/2 tsp baking powder
1/8 tsp salt
1 cup milk
1 tbsp vanilla
2 tbsps caraway seeds

Cream the margarine, butter and sugar. Add eggs one at a time, beating well after each addition. Then stir together the flour, baking powder and salt; add to creamed mixture alternately with milk. Add vanilla, then caraway seeds. Spoon mixture into greased Bundt pan. Bake at 325°F for 1 hour or until done.

Michaela squinted, struggling to see through the impenetrable darkness. Everyone looked toward the Elders, but she knew Brody Carter still watched her. Michaela could feel the power of his gaze. Its heat. Its strength. And something that felt strangely like anger, though he had no reason to have any emotion toward her. Strangers from different worlds, brought together beneath the heavy silver moon on a night made for hell itself. That was their only connection.

The second she finished that thought, she knew it was a lie. But she couldn't deal with it now. Not tonight. Not when her whole world balanced on the edge of destruction.

Willing her backbone to keep her upright, Michaela Doucet focused on the towering blaze of a roaring bonfire that rose from the far side of the clearing, its orange flames burning with maniacal zeal against the inky black curtain of the night. Many of the Lycans had already shifted into their preternatural shapes, their fur-covered bodies standing like monstrous shadows at the edges of the forest as they waited with restless expectancy for her brother.

Her nineteen-year-old brother, Max, had been attacked by a rogue werewolf—a Lycan who preyed upon humans for food. Max had been bitten in the attack, which meant he was no longer human, but a breed of creature that existed between the two worlds of man and beast, much like the Bloodrunners themselves.

The Elders parted, and two hulking shapes emerged from the trees. In their wolf forms, the Lycans stood over seven feet tall, their legs bent at an odd angle as they stalked forward. They each held a thick chain that had been wound around their inside wrists, the twin lengths leading back into the shadows. The Lycans had taken no more than a few steps when they jerked on the chains, and her brother appeared.

Bound like an animal.

Biting at her trembling lower lip, she glanced left, then right, surprised to see that others had joined her. Now the Bloodrunners and their family and friends stood as a united force against the Silvercrest pack, which had yet to accept the fact that something sinister was eating away at its foundation—something that would rip down the protective walls that separated their world from the humans'. It occurred to Michaela that loyalties were being announced tonight—a separation made between those who would stand with the Runners in their fight against the rogues and those who blindly supported the pack's refusal to face reality. But all she could focus on was her brother. Max looked so hurt...so terrified.

"Leave him alone," she screamed, her soft-soled, black satin slip-ons struggling for purchase in the damp earth as she rushed toward Max, only to find herself lifted off the ground when a hard, heavily muscled arm clamped around her waist from behind, pulling her clear off her feet. "Dammit, let me down!" she snarled, unable to take her eyes off her brother as the golden-eyed Lycan kicked him.

Mindless with heartache and rage, Michaela clawed at the arm holding her, kicking her heels against whatever part of her captor's legs she could reach. "Stop it," a deep, husky voice grunted in her ear. "You're not helping him by losing it. I give you my word he'll survive the ceremony, but you have to keep it together."

"Nooooo!" she screamed, too hysterical to listen to reason. "You're monsters! All of you! Look what you've done to him! How dare you! *How dare you!*"

The arm tightened with a powerful flex of muscle, cinching her waist. Her breath sucked in on a sharp, wailing gasp.

"Shut up before you get both yourself and your brother killed. I will *not* let that happen. Do you understand me?" her captor growled, shaking her so hard that her teeth clicked together. "Do you understand me, Doucet?"

"Dammit," she cried, stricken as she watched one of the guards grab Max by his hair. Around them Lycans huffed and growled as they watched the spectacle, while others outright howled for the show to begin.

"That's enough!" the voice seethed in her ear. "They'll tear you apart before you even reach him, and I'll be damned if I'm going to stand here and watch you die."

Suddenly, through the haze of fear and agony and outrage in her mind, she finally recognized who'd caught her. *Brody.*

He held her in his arms, her body locked against his powerful form, her back to the burning heat of his chest. A low, keening sound of anguish tore through her, and her head dropped forward as hoarse sobs of pain ripped from her throat. "Let me go. I have to help him. *Please*," she begged brokenly, knowing only that she needed to get to Max. "Let me go, Brody."

He muttered something against her hair, his breath warm against her scalp, and Michaela could have sworn it was a single word…. But she must have heard wrong. She was too upset. Too furious. Too terrified. She must be out of her mind.

Because it sounded as if he'd quietly snarled the word *never.*

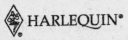

HARLEQUIN®

American ★ Romance®

Three Boys and a Baby

When Ella Garvey's eight-year-old twins and
their best friend, Dillon, discover an abandoned
baby girl, they fear she will be put in jail—
or worse! They decide to take matters into their
own hands and run away. Luckily the outlaws are
found quickly…and Ella finds a second chance
at love—with Dillon's dad, Jackson.

LOOK FOR

Three Boys and a Baby

BY

LAURA MARIE ALTOM

*Available May
wherever you buy books.*

LOVE, HOME & HAPPINESS

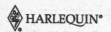
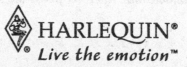

REQUEST YOUR FREE BOOKS!
2 FREE NOVELS PLUS 2
FREE GIFTS!

Heart, Home & Happiness!

YES! Please send me 2 FREE Harlequin American Romance® novels and my 2 FREE gifts (gifts are worth about $10). After receiving them, if I don't wish to receive any more books, I can return the shipping statement marked "cancel." If I don't cancel, I will receive 4 brand-new novels every month and be billed just $4.24 per book in the U.S. or $4.99 per book in Canada, plus 25¢ shipping and handling per book and applicable taxes, if any*. That's a savings of close to 15% off the cover price! I understand that accepting the 2 free books and gifts places me under no obligation to buy anything. I can always return a shipment and cancel at any time. Even if I never buy another book from Harlequin, the two free books and gifts are mine to keep forever.

154 HDN EEZK   354 HDN EEZV

Name	(PLEASE PRINT)	
Address		Apt. #
City	State/Prov.	Zip/Postal Code

Signature (if under 18, a parent or guardian must sign)

Mail to the **Harlequin Reader Service**:
IN U.S.A.: P.O. Box 1867, Buffalo, NY 14240-1867
IN CANADA: P.O. Box 609, Fort Erie, Ontario L2A 5X3

Not valid to current subscribers of Harlequin American Romance books.

Want to try two free books from another line?
Call 1-800-873-8635 or visit www.morefreebooks.com.

* Terms and prices subject to change without notice. N.Y. residents add applicable sales tax. Canadian residents will be charged applicable provincial taxes and GST. This offer is limited to one order per household. All orders subject to approval. Credit or debit balances in a customer's account(s) may be offset by any other outstanding balance owed by or to the customer. Please allow 4 to 6 weeks for delivery. Offer available while quantities last.

Your Privacy: Harlequin is committed to protecting your privacy. Our Privacy Policy is available online at www.eHarlequin.com or upon request from the Reader Service. From time to time we make our lists of customers available to reputable third parties who may have a product or service of interest to you. If you would prefer we not share your name and address, please check here. ☐

HAR08

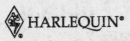

HARLEQUIN®

American ★ Romance®

COMING NEXT MONTH

#1209 THE FAMILY NEXT DOOR by Jacqueline Diamond
Harmony Circle

Josh Lorenz knows he's the last person Diane Bittner wants for a neighbor. But their preteen daughters have a different opinion. And when the girls start playing matchmaker for their clashing parents, Josh and Diane have to decide what really matters. Reliving the mistakes of the past? Or planning their future—together.

#1210 THE BEST MAN'S BRIDE by Lisa Childs
The Wedding Party

Colleen McCormick didn't expect to fall in love at her sister's wedding...and never dreams sexy best man Nick Jameson feels the same way! Then the bride bails, and Colleen and Nick are torn by divided loyalties. With the town of Cloverville up in arms, the cynical Nick must decide if he trusts in love enough to make Colleen the best man's bride.

#1211 THREE BOYS AND A BABY by Laura Marie Altom

When Ella Garvey's eight-year-old twins and their best friend Dillon discover an abandoned baby girl, they fear she will be put in jail—or worse! They take matters into their own hands and run away with the baby. Luckily the *outlaws* are found quickly...and Ella finds a second chance at love—with Dillon's dad, Jackson.

#1212 THE MOMMY BRIDE by Shelley Galloway
Motherhood

An unexpected pregnancy and a thirteen-year-old with an attitude complicate matters when Claire Grant falls for Dr. Ty Slattery. Claire has had a rocky past, making her wary of trusting anyone. But can the good doctor convince her—and her son—that together they can be a family?

www.eHarlequin.com

HARCNM0408